CTBT
India and the Nuclear Test Ban Treaty

CTBT
India and the Nuclear Test Ban Treaty

by
DR. SAVITA PANDE
Institute of Defence Studies and Analyses

Foreword by
AIR COMMODORE JASJIT SINGH
AVSM, VrC, VM, IAF (Retd.)

SIDDHI BOOKS
Imprint of
COSMO PUBLICATIONS
1996 NEW DELHI

First Cosmo Edition 1996
First Published: October 1996

© The Institute of Defense Studies and Analyses, New Delhi

All rights reserved. No part of this publication may be reproduced, stored in a retrieval system, or transmitted in any form or by any means, electronic, mechanical, photo-copying, recording or otherwise, without the prior permission of Cosmo Publications.

ISBN 81-7020-754-1

Nuclear-India. India-Nuclear-Testing. CTBT. Comprehensive Test Ban Treaty. Treaty-India-CTBT. Internationsl Law-India. Institute for Defense Studies and Analyses. Pande, Savita.

Manufactured in India

Published by:
MRS. RANI KAPOOR
For **SIDDHI BOOKS**
Imprint of
COSMO PUBLICATIONS
For **GENESIS PUBLISHING PVT. LTD.**
24-B, Ansari Road,
Darya Ganj,
New Delhi-110002. INDIA

Typeset by:
Manav Computer House
Delhi

Printed at:
Mehra Offset Press
Delhi

Contents

Foreword	*vii*
Historical Background	1
Test Ban Negotiations till 1980	21
The Second Cold War	43
Prelude to Current Phase of Negotiations	75
Crafting a CTBT	101
India's Response	167
Epilogue	221

Foreword

A Flawed Treaty

By

Air Commodore Jasjit Singh
Director
Institute for Defence Studies & Analyses

It is one of the ironies of realpolitik that India sought a nuclear test ban for the last 42 years but is now unable to sign the treaty when it is in its final shape and will, in fact, move to block its transmittal from the Conference on Disarmament(CD) at Geneva to UN General Assembly for signatures. The former decision arose from the failure of the draft treaty to meet the criteria of the negotiating mandate directed by the UN and an absence of any commitment to disarmament, while the second step is being necessitated by the Entry into Force clause insisted upon by some countries for diverse and questionable motivations.

The United States (which used to oppose similar resolutions in the past) co-sponsored with India the UN General Assembly's unanimously adopted resolution in 1993 calling for a *comprehensive* test ban treaty which would "effectively contribute" to the twin goal of nuclear non-proliferation "in all aspects", (that is, horizontal and vertical, qualitative and quantitative), as well as the "process of nuclear disarmament". The negotiating mandate adopted by the CD in January 1994 also specified the same language and objectives. President Clinton had joined Prime Minister Narasimha Rao in calling for the twin goals of non-proliferation and disarmament in 1994, and so had other heads of states. The treaty draft that has now emerged at the CD fails completely in meeting the terms of negotiating mandate.

The treaty will allow sub-critical tests and computer simulation to design, fabricate, and test new types of warheads. The treaty will, in reality, legitimise a new qualitative arms race. There is also no provision to ban transfer of proven nuclear weapon design and technology by a nuclear weapon state to another state. What we are seeing is a treaty which, like the NPT, will be a licence to proliferate vertically without effectively banning horizontal proliferation.

The treaty fails to meet the second goal of the negotiating mandate totally since it does not even attempt to contribute to the "process of disarmament". In fact the five weapon states (and the two dozen protected by nuclear umbrella) wish to avoid any commitment to disarmament except in the vaguest terms less binding than Article VI of NPT (which remains unactioned).

In trying to understand the Indian position with regard to the Comprehensive Test Ban Treaty (CTBT) negotiated at the CD, it is necessary to note that this is a position for which extensive widespread consensus exists in the country. Some people have even described the government position as one which is propelled by the weight of public opinion, at the elite as well as the broader public levels. Two factors have been responsible for the evolution of this consensus. One concerns some core fundamental issues where nuclear disarmament is central to the Indian position; and the second relates to the technical and operational aspects of the treaty in terms of its comprehensiveness and verification means and methods. India's position that it will not sign the treaty "in its present form" is based on what it sees as central issues related to both aspects, although the issue of binding commitments to nuclear disarmament is more central. This is also one area where there has been no willingness on the part of the nuclear weapon states to even discuss, leave alone negotiate, with India. On the other hand, in recent years the United States has formally adopted a policy of "cap, reduce, and eliminate" India's nuclear capabilities without any concern about the security challenges faced by India although the US supports a "robust defence" capability fo r India.

The CTBT directly affects the five nuclear weapon states and the three "threshold states" (I ndia, Israel, and Pakistan). The remaining non-nuclear weapon states are already committed under the NPT to indefinitely abstain from nuclear tests. China and Russia have serious difficulties with the asymmetric capping that the CTBT will achieve and the technical operational aspects like monitoring and verification procedures which would eventually require many compromises. Meanwhile, China, Britain, and Russia also have been searching for a way out of the CTBT, making it contingent to India's ratification of a treaty which India has already said it will not sign.[1]

Negotiating Mandate

The critics of the Indian position claim that a commitment to elimination of nuclear weapons is not relevant since the CTBT is only meant to stop testing and is not a vehicle for disarmament. This posture would have been more credible if even a parallel process of disarmament had been allowed to commence. But it is relevant to note that the mandate adopted by the CD on January 25, 1994 required it to negotiate a treaty which would "effectively contribute" to the twin goals of "nuclear non-proliferation in all its aspects", (that is, vertical and horizontal, qualitative and quantitative), as well as "the process of (global) nuclear disarmament".

The mandate had grown out of the UN General Assembly resolution 49/70 on the CTBT (passed without a vote on December 15, 1993) which also sought these twin goals while placing greater stress on disarmament. India had been one of the original co-sponsors of the resolution, later to be joined by the USA. India's then Foreign Secretary, JN Dixit, has stated that at the time of co-sponsoring the resolution in 1993, the US and other nuclear weapon states had assured India that disarmament will be an important goal of the CTBT negotiations.[2] Within four months after the CD adopted the mandate, President Clinton and Indian Prime Minister Narasimha Rao issued a joint statement in Washington on May 14, 1994 endorsing the pursuit of both non-proliferation and disarmament. Unfortunately, the White House spokesman stated later that he was not aware of any such statement.[3] Similar commitments were also given by other heads of states.

In spite of the CD's mandate, the treaty proposed by the Ad-hoc Committee at Geneva fails to meet some basic criteria even in respect of non-proliferation. Firstly, it will not stop vertical proliferation. On the other hand, there is every reason to believe that it sets the framework for a new qualitative arms race since it does not prohibit non-explosive testing or computer generated design and tests of new weapons. The US has clearly asserted and indicated plans to "Maintain the capability to design, fabricate and certify new warheads" although no production of new warheads may be involved (but this can change any time).[4] While the negotiations for a CTBT were in progress, the US finalised an agreement to share data and technology with France to help the latter make qualitative improvements and newer weapons in future without explosive testing. During the same period, the US also cynically awarded a $94 million contract to IBM for supply (by 1998) of ultra super computers to help design and test (without explosion) new nuclear weapons. Energy Secretary Hazel O'Leary reportedly predicted that this would enable scientists to solve many technological questions that now can be answered only by physical underground testing.[5] US Department of Energy's Science Based Stockpile Stewardship (SBSS) programme will maintain both nuclear warheads and weapon designers indefinitely. This is also why France conducted a series of tests, China continued to do so, and the US has agreed to provide France with technological assistance to sustain better arsenals.[6] The US has similar arrangements with the UK, and had even offered simulation technology to China in 1994. China's goals of authorising peaceful nuclear explosions under the CTBT are, no doubt, driven by the intention of acquiring data for future qualitative improvements.

Qualitative improvements by the five nuclear weapon states will continue in the absence of a ban on subcritical testing and simulation processes and techniques. One of the original goals of the Indian proposal for a test ban was to stop the nuclear arms race. As we know, the nuclear arms race was instead pursued viciously by five countries. It is indeed ironic that this race, which appeared to have stopped with the end of a Cold War, now is likely to be triggered and legitimised by the nature of the so-called CTBT.

The CTBT must also be viewed in the context of other developments. The US is planning to deploy antiballistic missile systems and is negotiating demarcation definitions of the ABM Treaty with Russia to expand the scope of such a system. The plan to deploy such system in East Asia (where Japan has already agreed to cooperate) is likely to lead to China pressing ahead with qualitative and quantitative improvements and expansion of its arsenal. This appears to have been the reason for China seeking exemption for "peaceful nuclear explosions" which could be utilised for data collection for newer warhead designs. While the CTBT is not meant to specifically deal with this issue, India can hardly ignore the implications of such developments.

Secondly, the treaty will prohibit explosive testing, but will not stop a non-nuclear weapon state (party or non-party to the NPT) from acquiring weapons. Iraq and North Korea have already demonstrated the inability of existing regimes like the NPT to stop a member state from pursuing a clandestine weapons programme and even obtaining technology and material from nuclear weapon states members of the NPT. The dangers to international peace and security of untested nuclear weapons are not any less than those of tested ones. Iraq's weapons would not have been any less credible without a test. Pakistan's bomb is seen as a credible threat by the decision-makers in India. This is because the target country cannot assume that an untested nuclear warhead will not explode if used. The user would only need to increase the number of weapons used for greater assurance if there is any uncertainty that a warhead may not work. It is useful to remember that the Hiroshima bomb was untested.

Thirdly, the treaty being finalised has no provision to address the problem posed by the transfer of tested designs by a nuclear weapon state to another country. Western reports have been asserting for many years that Pakistan received a tested design for its bomb from China. More recently, China was accused by the United States of transferring nuclear weapons technology to

FOREWORD xiii

Pakistan when the ring magnets were supplied in gross violation of Articles I and III of the NPT which forbid such transfers. The inability or unwillingness of the US-led international community to take action has seriously weakened the already inadequate non-proliferation regime.

As regards the second aspect of the mandate, that is, the disarmament aspect, the nuclear weapon states led by the US have been making sure that there is no linkage to disarmament in the treaty, nor has a parallel process been allowed to be established. For India, the issue of global disarmament is crucial. The arsenals of the five nuclear weapon states have been the prime factor for the pressures on security of other countries, nearly two dozen of which have sought solutions through nuclear umbrellas of the weapon states. Disarmament approach is the only viable way of looking at the role of nuclear weapons in the 21st century.

Nuclear weapons have reinforced an iniquitous world order, especially since the five weapon states are also the permanent members of the UN Security Council. Democracy at national levels cannot be embedded on a durable basis without democratisation of inter-state relations. Nuclear disarmament will be a major step toward a more equitous international order. Unfortunately, the treaty being finalised at the CD is nothing more than a partial test ban treaty, and fails by a wide margin to meet the requirements of the mandate that the CD had set for itself over two years ago.

Comprehensive or Partial Test Ban?

Another issue is the comprehensiveness of the treaty. The nuclear weapon states have reached various levels of technological capabilities to enable them to keep improving their arsenals and develop newer weapons. Like the 1992 draft Defence Guidance document showed, the US aim is to ensure that no rival state will emerge with capabilities to challenge the US at a future date. This has been a major factor in its shift (in 1993) from a vehement opposition of a CTBT for decades to a high profile support for it now as an arms control and counter proliferation measure. Since the US is ahead of others, it seeks now to freeze further qualitative development of other nuclear arsenals (especially China and Russia) in pursuit of its national interests besides "capping" capabilities of countries like India and locking in those like Japan. But the qualitative improvements in the nuclear arsenal of the weapon states could continue if the treaty is not what it claims to be ___ *comprehensive*. The concept of a CTBT is to stop testing of nuclear weapons which would also stop design and development of any new weapons. Not all steps required to make it comprehensive can be effectively verifiable internationally. To cover such cases, political commitments need to be included in the treaty terms.

Verification of such a treaty must be vested in an international system managed by the international community on the basis similar to that of the IAEA, if not by IAEA itself. There must not be any role for autonomous "national technical means" in this process. There is a risk that every time a tubewell is bored in a country, claims on the basis of national technical means (satellite pictures etc.) can be made by another nation that "on site verification" is necessary! The international hype last December about India planning to carry out a nuclear test is an example of the implications of alleged use and mis-use of information from national technical means of great powers.

The Core Issue

As noted earlier, the negotiating mandate for the CTBT required it to effectively contribute to the "process of disarmament". It is toward this end that India proposed amendments. Unfortunately the main players at the CD displayed total contempt in not even deigning to discuss this aspect leave alone hold negotiations on the subject of the CTBT's role in disarmament, especially the amendment proposed by India in pursuance of the negotiating mandate adopted by the CD.

Unfortunately, India's stand on nuclear disarmament has been grossly misunderstood over the years. It is, therefore, important to examine whether India is merely "posturing", being "moralistic", or are some core fundamental issues and interests dictating its policy?

Nuclear disarmament has emerged as the core issue driving India's position on the CTBT. For five decades India has been at the forefront of efforts and demands for total elimination of nuclear weapons. This position had been supported, at the UN and outside it, by the majority of the international community and some nuclear weapon states during the Cold War. Peace movements had been extremely active especially in the 1980s in seeking nuclear disarmament. But with the end of the Cold War, the risk of nuclear war having reduced, the international community became more sanguine about the dangers of nuclear weapons although the doomsday clock was shifted back only a few minutes. A paradox has grown where nuclear weapons, justified for more than four decades in the context of the Cold War, now are sought to be retained for undefined and ephemeral threats because there is no Cold War. It is in this context that the nuclear weapon states agreed to negotiate a Comprehensive Test Ban Treaty ___ something that they had strongly resisted for forty years.

There are four central reasons why nuclear disarmament is a strategic goal for India. *Firstly,* there is the issue of moral and ethical basis for this demand. Nuclear weapons are the worst form of weapons of mass destruction. Indians do not believe that morality and fundamental human values must be necessarily sacrificed at the altar of national interests. Linked to the moral principle is the issue of legality and legitimacy. The indefinite extension of the NPT, which is the only international treaty legitimising nuclear weapons, and especially the efforts of some nuclear weapon states to ensure that no linkage with disarmament is established in spite of the commitments in the treaty itself, and of others like China which set about testing nuclear weapons within hours of giving a commitment to exercise "the utmost restraint" in this regard has influenced Indian thinking deeply. India has been seeking a convention to outlaw the use and threat of use of nuclear weapons — a resolution at the UN supported by an overwhelming majority of states year after year since 1978, especially during the Cold War. Even now, the International Court of Justice has ruled that the use of nuclear weapons is not consistent with the laws of armed conflict that a civilised world has otherwise adopted.

Secondly, nuclear disarmament will be a major factor enhancing international peace and security. The argument that nuclear weapons had kept the peace during the Cold War is fatally flawed since the concept, taken to its logical application, would sanction nuclear weapons for most if not all sovereign states in the world. And so is the view that the weapons need to be retained in future, even if only by the nuclear five. Nuclear weapons use would affect not only the combatant countries but large parts of the world.

Thirdly, nuclear weapons need to be eliminated if we are to move toward a more equitable international order. Democracy at the national level cannot be sustained as a core principle without movement toward greater democratisation of the international order. Unfortunately, nuclear weapons have sustained an inequitable order by creating a powerful distinction between the haves and the have-nots. Nuclear weapons have been legitimised with the five countries who also are the permanent members of the UN Security Council with veto powers. This has created a nexus between iniquitous power based substantively on nuclear weapons as the ultimate arbiter of hegemony and influence on one side, and geopolitical framework of an international order reflecting the now outdated power equations of an earlier colonial era, on the other.

Fourthly, the issue of national security remains central to Indian policy. There is a need to recognise that India's strategic and security interests are served better if there are no nuclear weapons that can impinge on India's security calculus. Nuclear disarmament, therefore, is not only a moral/ethical principle for us, and a necessity for international peace and security, but *an imperative for national security*. Pakistan, in a non-nuclear environment, would pose a lesser security challenge in view of India's size and potential. The divergence in relative capabilities, in reality, has been growing in our favour during the past three decades. It is for this very reason that Pakistan, in an effort to neutralise India's intrinsic conventional superiority, has acquired nuclear weapons. Contrary to popular belief, in a conventional military scenario, India would be in a better position to defend itself if a situation like that in 1962 develops in relation to China also. There is finite limit to the quality and quantity of force that China can deploy on the Himalayan borders and sustain it for operations. We have shorter logistic lines. Geography and the very nature of terrain dictates that Indian air power (not used in 1962, essentially on US advice) will remain superior and able to influence the ground battle, unless we allow the balance to alter. In any case, if the defence planners perceive existing force levels to be inadequate, raising additional mountain Divisions should be a less demanding alternative for a country with 930 million population! It is the nuclear factor that places us at a gross disadvantage on the two key frontiers.

Nuclear disarmament, therefore, is fundamental to our strategic and security interests. The fact that this also coincides with our principles and the moral/ethical approach to nuclear weapons only enhances the need for nuclear disarmament for international peace and security as well as our own. Pragmatic assessment indicates that such disarmament cannot be accepted unilaterally (and hence the position that India will not accept any restraint on its policy in the absence of a commitment to disarmament) or in a narrow regional or sub-regional framework. It would be naive to ask or expect China to disarm in the absence of a larger process. The only viable solution to our security concerns related to nuclear weapons lies in pursuing total elimination of nuclear weapons from national arsenals. This is also the rationale why our concept of a CTBT has been linked to elimination of nuclear weapons from the time Prime Minister Jawaharlal Nehru called for it in April 1954.

Scope for Nuclear Disarmament

A view is being propagated that in linking the CTBT to nuclear disarmament, India has now changed its stand. Unfortunately, people who choose to ignore facts of history, for whatever reasons, also ignore weight of evidence that India's demands for a nuclear test ban treaty over the past four decades has been linked to nuclear disarmament. If the Indian position appears more unambiguously linked to time bound programme (although not any more than the formal proposal to the UN at the Special Session on Disarmament in 1988) it is because the international community, for the first time, is now seriously negotiating a comprehensive test ban treaty and the terms of the treaty are important for those who wish to be committed to it. It is, of course, good to see people quoting Jawaharlal Nehru to us today; but they are careful not to mention that Nehru, when he called (in 1954) for halting nuclear tests clearly said that this was to "Standstill" (that is, some sort of a moratorium) while disarmament is pursued.

India had first formally sought a comprehensive ban on nuclear testing in April 1954. This was unambiguously stated to be a proposal for a "Standstill Agreement" pending "discontinuance of production and stockpiling" of nuclear weapons.[7] But the nuclear weapon states have not even been willing to standstill through a moratorium, leave alone stop all testing for all times. Of course, if India's call had been listened to at that time, there would have been no nuclear arms race, there would have been a maximum of two nuclear weapon states with no scope for qualitative improvements, and we would not have been faced with a nuclearised environment.

It is obvious that the CTBT in its present form fails to meet our fundamental interests and principles. This has also been the real problem with the NPT which did not fulfil the direction given by the unanimous resolution of the UN General Assembly on November 19, 1965. It may be recalled that India was at the forefront seeking an NPT since October 1964; but this, as the 1965 UN General Assembly resolution required, was to provide a treaty that leads to not only non-proliferation, but more important, forms the basis of disarmament which the negotiating process diluted substantively.[8] The NPT itself contains clauses, even if watered down in the process of negotiations, that require multilateral negotiations, in good faith, to achieve nuclear disarmament. Unfortunately, the disarmament provisions of the NPT have remained unimplemented more than 25 years after the treaty came into force. On the other hand, while seeking permanent extension of the NPT last year, the nuclear weapon states (especially the US) went out of their way to ensure that no commitments were made with regard to disarmament. The nuclear weapon states have refused to be accountable for their violation of the NPT clauses; and hence the NPT review conferences have not been able to issue an agreed final statement in 1990 and 1995.

Since the NPT is not allowed to be a vehicle for disarmament even under its diffused provisions, the disarmament linkage in the CTBT becomes even more important. These cannot be adequate only with a stronger language in the preamble. The Cold War used to be cited in justification for nuclear weapons, but the Cold War has been over for five years. As we stand on the threshold of the 21st century, decisive movement toward total elimination of nuclear weapons becomes even more important than ever before. The international community has concluded treaties to eliminate the other two categories of weapons of mass destruction which stand out as models for abolition of nuclear weapons. There is no justifiable reason for tardiness and opposition to total elimination of the third category. The argument that the world will be unsafe without nuclear weapons is only meant to further the narrow self interests of the nuclear weapon states and their allies. Competent people like former US Defence Secretary and senior military commanders in the report of the committee chaired by General Andrew Goodpaster have already argued that US security will be enhanced with total elimination of nuclear weapons.[9] They have recommended a phased programme of disarmament which could be achieved in a couple of decades. Australian Prime Minister Mr. Paul Keating, while announcing the setting up of the Canberra

FOREWORD

Commission of experts to work out a plan for total elimination of nuclear weapons had stated "I believe that a world free of nuclear weapons is now feasible."[10] He went on to say "We want the nuclear weapon states to carry out their commitments to the elimination of their nuclear stockpiles by adopting a systematic process to achieve that result."

The nuclear weapon states have been resisting all attempts at getting them to commit to disarmament. India's approach is considered unrealistic without ascribing any reason why it is so. At the same time, strong assertions are made that notable steps toward disarmament have been made with Start I and II which will reduce the two primary nuclear powers' arsenals to 6,500 warheads. This itself indicates a false picture since the actual number of warheads with the US alone after START II implementation would be over 8,500! Assuming the same number for Russia (although the number is likely to be higher), the world nuclear arsenal at the end of existing plans to reduce warheads would still leave around 19,000 nuclear warheads with no plan to reduce them any further and no commitment even to do so. Past commitments, like Article VI in the NPT, have been ignored completely since even negotiations under this Article, agreed upon in 1968, have yet to start. To remind the international community of this obligation, the World Court has now ruled unanimously on July 8 that "There exists an obligation to pursue in good faith and bring to a conclusion negotiations leading to nuclear disarmament in all aspects under strict international control."[11]

India has been charged with lack of realism in asking for disarmament under a time bound programme. Experts believe that a time-frame of 10 years is realistic. President Gorbachev of the USSR had called for total elimination of nuclear weapons in 10-12 years when the global arsenal had over 57,000 warheads. The figure is already coming down to half that number, and the Cold War ended five years ago. It is significant that the President of Pugwash Conference on Science and World Affairs and Nobel Peace Prize winner, eminent nuclear scientist (an erstwhile member of the Manhattan project), Professor Joseph Rotblat in his Nobel Speech in December 1995 asserted that, "We have the technical means to create a Nuclear Weapon Free World *in about a decade*". (Emphasis added) Other Pugwash scientists believe it is feasible to dismantle nuclear warheads in about 10 years, and that the goal of global nuclear disarmament can be achieved in 20-30 years. It is clear, therefore, that the nuclear weapon states (and their allies under the nuclear weapon umbrellas) are adamant in retaining nuclear weapon into an undefined future basically to perpetuate nuclear hegemony.

On the other hand, if the present language proposed by India is found to be unacceptable by the weapons states, are they prepared to accept any other language that commits the international community firmly to nuclear disarmament which they all claim is a goal? But it is clear that they do not want to make any such commitment or honour the commitments made earlier. The crucial question that we need to be clear about in our mind is: what sort of treaty does the international community want, and what sort of treaty can India sign? *If the CTBT fails to meet the fundamental criteria of being an unambiguous step toward nuclear disarmament, India could hardly be expected to sign it,* even if India was acknowledged as a nuclear weapon state.

National Security Imperative

India's nuclear policy has been shaped by the factor of nuclearisation of its security environment since the early 1960s. The beginning of many of India's non-proliferation and disarmament initiatives can be traced to that period. While China-India relations have been improving in the recent years, there are major uncertainties about the future strategic scenario. China is deeply engaged in qualitative and quantitative build up of its nuclear arsenal. This modernisation is likely to increase in future. It needs to be recalled that China carried out a nuclear test within hours of giving a commitment (during the NPT extension conference in 1995) that required the utmost restraint in carrying out nuclear explosions. It has continued to test since then at sites less than the 1,000km from India. According to reports, US Defence Secretary stated that China has been providing nuclear weapon technology to Pakistan in recent past. China has also supplied nuclear capable missiles for delivery. According to Professor Christoph Bluth, "In order to contain the perceived threat from India, China entered into technical co-operation with Pakistan to the extent that the USA alleged that China sold Pakistan a nuclear weapon design." [12] The US Secretary of Defence, Dr. William Perry, speaking at the US Foreign Policy Association in January 1995 after a visit to India, acknowledged that India's concerns are related to China and the wider issues, rather than Pakistan. India has clearly expressed its concerns regarding nuclear weapon technology cooperation between China and Pakistan.

It is significant that China, in insisting that the CTBT must be subject to India's ratification, for the first time, has taken a public posture seeking to curtail India's options. This is obviously with the aim of keeping India at disadvantageous position permanently. China and India signed an agreement in September 1993 for maintaining peace and tranquillity on the borders based on the principle of "mutual and equal security". But the existing nuclear asymmetry, especially without any commitment to nuclear disarmament, is inconsistent with this principle. Russia also seeks to apply the current CTBT to India. This may well be with the expectations that India will have to rely to a greater measure on Moscow in dealing with China in future. The 1971 treaty of friendship between USSR and India is relevant from this perspective. The US, now insisting India's ratification of a treaty that India has said does not meet its core concerns, may also be hoping that a disadvantaged India would have to rely on the USA in future.

Since the international community does not want to start the process of nuclear disarmament at this stage, India has to pursue its national security policies keeping this factor in mind. This also has to be seen in the context of the stated policy of the United States to "cap, reduce, and eliminate" India's nuclear capabilities. The US has continued to apply undue pressure on India on missile and nuclear issues even after India did not do anything negative to US interests in the NPT extension process. India continues to be treated as a virtual "rogue" state in terms of export control laws and a range of commercial activities important for development. The US is believed to have been applying pressure to block the Russian supply of two nuclear power reactors which are necessary to build adequate power generation capabilities so that economic and industrial development proceeds unhindered. These and many more factors are leading to a serious reassessment of the fundamentals of Indian nuclear policy and posture.

There is no conceivable political goal or situation that in the Indian perceptions would require India to have nuclear weapons to threaten another country first. This is why it has been easy for us to demand a global "no-first-use" commitment, to unilaterally assure such a posture in 1990 (which requires to be formally articulated), and propose to Pakistan in January 1994 a bilateral agreement for no-first-use (of 'nuclear capabilities', since both countries claim that they do not possess weapons). The only contingency in which India would require nuclear weapons is to deter another country from holding out a threat of use or possibly even use of nuclear weapons against India. And this would require minimum deterrence in the worst case, while "recessed deterrence" should be adequate for all scenarios less adverse than that. This capability, therefore, becomes a critical minimum national security imperative.

A CTBT, even clearly linked to disarmament, of course, would prohibit India from testing and improving its capabilities in future if it signs the treaty. Unlike other threshold states like Israel and Pakistan, India had carried out a (peaceful) nuclear explosion 22 years ago. But it has not followed up with any other test. Signing the CTBT would not close India's nuclear option. But it will define the type of deterrent capability that India can acquire. The issue of the type of deterrent India would need must be seen from the perspective of the reason why we need nuclear weapons, if at all. India does not require nuclear weapons to enhance its prestige and status, although nuclear weapons have constituted the currency of international power for half a century. India is already one of the leading half a dozen centres of power in the world. We recognise that our status, in the final analysis, will be governed really by how we deal with challenges and solve our problems rather than mere possession of nuclear weapons. The issue, therefore, is not so much that India wants to avoid a commitment of not testing in future, but more of the signing away the sovereign right to do so, especially for qualitative improvements that may be necessary at a future date in a world where the weapon states are not willing even to consider moving toward elimination of their arsenals.

It is clear that the nuclear weapon states advocate a step by step approach, but do not wish to take the first step and make any commitment toward total elimination of nuclear weapons. "Under such circumstances, it is natural that our national security considerations become a key factor in our decision making. Our capability is demonstrated but, as a matter of policy, we exercise restraint. Countries around us continue their nuclear programmes, either openly or in a clandestine manner. In such an environment, India cannot accept any restraint on its capability if other countries remain unwilling to accept the obligation to eliminate their nuclear weapons."[13]

India will obviously continue to work for the goal of achieving a nuclear weapon-free world, even if it remains a long-term proposition. In the meantime, we are left with no alternative but to take this reality into account in formulating our policy responses in the short and near term perspective. India will not be willing to accept any restraints on its nuclear policy in this regard. If we sign a CTBT without a linkage to disarmament, then there is little prospect of our being able to influence progress toward our fundamental interests of a non-nuclear environment at a future date. A CTBT linked to disarmament in an unambiguous way would be worth giving up the option to test in future. Anything less would not. If this linkage is not established now, it will be more difficult to do so in the proposed treaty to stop production of fissile material for weapons purposes in future which is slated for negotiations at the CD.

The End Game

The negotiations at Geneva were abandoned rather pre-emptorily by the Chairman on June 28 although many of the key states like China and Russia were wanting to continue negotiations to hammer out their differences. On June 20, India had stated its position that it will not sign the treaty "in its present form." The Chairman's draft text at that stage also included the clause making the treaty's entry into force contingent upon the ratification of the treaty by 37 countries on whose territories the International Monitoring System facilities were located. This would have made India's accession to the treaty a pre-condition to its entry into force. India, not wanting to block the treaty through this process, also announced the withdrawal of its facilities from the International Monitoring System. However, India made it clear that it would continue to remain part of the CD in further negotiations of the CTBT. This was obviously to convey that our problem was not the principle of a CTBT, but the text in its present form.

India's balanced and dignified stand resulted in many of the inner contradictions among the affected parties coming to the fore. At the same time some of the countries like China, Pakistan, Russia, and the UK sought to insist that India's ratification was essential for the treaty. The British diplomat, without explaining why his country would not support a commitment to nuclear disarmament, even went into a semi-hysterical undiplomatic posturing. The Chairman, before abandoning negotiations, dutifully produced another draft on the final day which listed the ratification of 44 countries (under another criterion) including India as essential for entry into force. This was an unprecedented step totally violating international treating making rules to include India in the list in spite of India having clearly indicated its position the previous week, of not signing the treaty. If it goes through, this will set a new precedent with far-reaching consequences where a majority of countries could negotiate an international treaty and make it applicable to one or more countries even if they are not willing to sign it, and subsequently threaten these countries with "measures" designed to obtain their acquiescence. In fact, those who support the entry into force clause in the form presented by Mr. Ramaker (which is neither a consensus draft, nor a negotiated one) also argue for a "step by step" approach to nuclear disarmament where the CTBT is seen as a first step. They would be well advised to follow their own prescription and adopt a step by step approach to the CTBT by countries that accept this draft, signing it as a first step rather than making it contingent on a country that had already stated that it will not sign. But Mr. Ramaker made it clear that he views the CTBT as relevant only to bring India into its fold since the five nuclear weapon states have already accepted stopping tests![14]

The United States had adopted a more relaxed view earlier looking for ratification by 40-65 countries and the five nuclear weapon states as the condition for the treaty to enter into force. However, in mid-July, the United States reversed its stand and decided to go along with the hard-liners seeking India's ratification as a precondition to bring CTBT into force. This gave rise to some views in India that Britain's high profile shrill posture was in fact only a front for US policy. However, this reversal in US stand has come under criticism in the United States where the *New York Times* and the *International Herald Tribune* in strong editorial comments castigated the administration for having "stumbled" in its hasty compromises which now put the treaty at risk and which may not now come into force at an early date.[15] Britain also contemptuously ignored the unanimous European Parliament resolution of July 19 asking it to moderate its position on the entry into force clause and asking all EU members to cooperate in an early and smooth finalisation of the CTBT. The European Parliament also asked Britain and India to "do their utmost to reach agreement on solving the conflict that has arisen" and urged the EU countries to "work for a less complicated entry into force provision which will allow the Treaty to enter into force at the earliest possible date."[16] The position taken by India would have, and could still allow

FOREWORD

easy and early passage of the CTBT and its entry into force.

On the other side, India's Foreign Minister, Shri I.K. Gujral made it clear in the parliament on July 15 that "Our approach will remain a responsible approach, but we have to safeguard our national interest. If other countries reach their own consensus, that is their own sovereign decision. We would expect that all countries respect our decision and ensure that the Treaty, with which we will not be associated, not impose any obligations on India." [17] He also made the Indian position explicit to the US Secretary of state, Mr. Warren Christopher, in their meeting at Jakarta after which he stated that "we have agreed to disagree."

As of mid-August it is clear that if the CD proceeds with retaining the entry into force clause as defined in Chairman Ramaker's draft of June 28, India will be left with no option but to oppose any consensus for the treaty at the CD invoking supreme national interest and the right to self defence sanctioned by the UN Charter. In essence, India would seek to block the entry into force clause. But since the treaty cannot be voted upon clause by clause, it would imply voting against the treaty text itself blocking the principle of consensus at the CD and hence transmittal of the treaty by the CD to the UN General Assembly. This may or may not block the treaty as such since other avenues could be found. But India will have to protest strongly against the blatant arm twisting and attempt at blackmail. India in fact made this position explicit at the CD on July 29,1996, and it also moved an amendment to the entry into force clause which requires a simple formula of ratification by 65 countries (like in the Chemical Weapons Convention) for the treaty to enter into force.

Already the attitudes in India are hardening against the coercive diplomacy of a handful of states which wish to retain nuclear weapons indefinitely, and do not actually want a CTBT, but do not display the moral courage to stand on their own feet while wanting to fire their guns on Indian shoulders. The real responsibility for blocking the treaty under such circumstances would rest not on India (which has already made it clear that it does not wish to block the treaty, but will not sign it in its present form), but on countries that insist on making the CTBT conditional to a patently illegal and perverse clause. Mr. Ramaker's second draft, supported by the US, China, Britain, and Russia, has shifted the central issue from the nature and substance of the treaty to issues of sovereignty and international norms. The way these get resolved will have a long-term implications on international peace and security, well beyond the CTBT.

Notes and References

1. Pakistan's position, as in the case of the NPT etc., has been predictably consistently dishonest, even if it apparently provides it diplomatic payoffs. The British position at Geneva surprised most Indians who tend to see it as one which seeks international limelight, even if momentarily, while protecting the perpetuation of its own nuclear arsenal.
2. *Indian Express*, April 16, 1996.
3. *PTI*, October 5, 1995.
4. Harold Smith (Assistant Secretary of Defense), "Assuring confidence in the US nuclear stockpile" cited in *USIA Wireless File*, May 31, 1996, p.19.
5. *Pioneer*, August 10, 1996.
6. *International Herald Tribune*, June 17, 1996.
7. UN *Official Records of the Disarmament Commission*, Supplement for April, May, and June, 1954, DC/44 and Corr.1. The proposal stated that,
   "Pending progress toward some solution, full or partial, in respect of the prohibition and elimination of these weapons

FOREWORD

of mass destruction, which the General Assembly has affirmed as its nearest desire, the Government would consider, among other steps to be taken forthwith, the following:

"(1) Some sort of, what may be called, "Standstill Agreement" in respect, at least, of these actual explosions ....."

8. India's proposal for the NPT was closely related to China's acquisition of nuclear weapons in 1964.
9. *An Evolving US Nuclear Posture*, Second Report of the Steering Committee, Project on Eliminating Weapons of Mass Destruction, Henry L. Stimson Center, Washington DC, December 1995.
10. P.J. Keating, Prime Minister of Australia. Speech given on the 50th Anniversary of the United Nations, October 24, 1995.
11. *Legality of the Threat or Use of Nuclear Weapons*, Advisory Opinion, Communique No. 96/23, July 8, 1996, International Court of Justice, The Hague.
12. Professor Christoph Bluth, "Beijing's attitude to arms control", *Jane's Intelligence Review*, July 1996, p.328.
13. Arundhati Ghosh, Permanent Representative of India at the Conference on Disarmament, in a statement at the Plenary Session, June 20, 1996.
14. Jaap Ramaker (Q&A), "Test Ban Pact is Doable", *International Herald Tribune*, July 1, 1996.
15. "A Weak Nuclear Deal", *International Herald Tribune*, August 2, 1996.
16. *Resolution on the Comprehensive Test Ban Treaty*, European Parliament, July 19, 1996.
17. IK Gujral, External Affairs Minister of India, in a suo moto statement to the Parliament, New Delhi, July 15, 1996.

Chapter 1
Historical Background

The roots of comprehensive test ban can be traced back to 1954 (March 1, to be precise) when an American nuclear test of a 15-megaton hydrogen bomb was conducted on Namu Island in the Bikini Atoll.[1] The test which was part of the series of nuclear tests called "Operation Castle" dramatically highlighted dangers of a radioactive fall-out. It had surpassed the estimated yield and caused severe fall-out beyond the restricted testing area.[2] Official statements confirmed the radioactive contamination of 28 Americans and 236 residents of the nearby Marthall Islands. Severe contamination of a Japanese fishing boat which returned to its home harbour two weeks later caught public attention since the crew had been exposed to such a high radiation that one of the members died.

It was in this background that in an address to the Indian Parliament on 2 April 1954, the then Prime Minister Pandit Jawaharlal Nehru called for an "immediate standstill" agreement by the two superpowers until the United Nations had elaborated a comprehensive disarmament agreement.[3] During the same month, other distinguished figures like Albert Schweitzer and Pope Pius XII called for the cessation of nuclear explosions.[4]

At the UN General Assembly in December 1954, India repeated its proposal for a total cessation of nuclear testing but did not put it to vote.[5] However, its proposal to establish a scientific committee to enquire into the effects of radiation was adopted unanimously.[6] The UN Committee on the 'Effects of Atomic Radiation', thus set up, reported ambiguously in 1958 that radiation could cause somatic and genetic effects, but that no such effects had been found. The Committee continued to meet and submitted several periodic reports.[7]

In 1955, the Soviet Union submitted a two-stage plan for the reduction of arms, which included in its first stage, the cessation of tests.[8] Despite a developing concern about nuclear weapons on the part of President Eisenhower, USA resisted international pressures and rejected the idea of a test ban. In October 1956, the Soviet Prime Minister Bulganin formally proposed the cessation of nuclear testing but dismissed any need for international verification of compliance, maintaining that these tests could be detected by national means.[9] The US Administration rejected the Bulganin proposal and also the UK proposal asking USA for "private discussions on test restrictions." This was done for two reasons: Firstly, international verification was regarded as indespensible. Secondly, USA was pursuing the strategy of military superiority, hence a cessation of tests could have enabled the USSR to catch up quantitatively. By contrast, Soviet leaders Khruschev and Bulganin adopted the test ban as a central item in their arms control agenda in mid-1955, but they offered this proposal as part of the package proposals.

In January 1957, USA submitted to the UN General Assembly a five-point plan which focussed on the cessation of production of nucelar weapons, and if this could be achieved, on the cessation of nuclear testing as well. This reflected the traditional US position, but was modified with a proposal calling for advance notice of nuclear tests (the same proposal was made earlier by Canada,

Japan and Norway).[10] During the course of discussion, the two superpowers continued their testing activities although public pressure was growing and countries like Japan and Germany sought cessation of tests. On 15 May 1957, UK tested its first thermonuclear device and reported that it had entered the select circle of full-fledged nuclear powers.[11] In the aftermath, UK opposed a test ban since it still maintained only a very small stockpile of four bombs and first wanted to develop it further. A similar position was held by France which was engaged in the development of its own arsenals.

The United Nations Subcommittee of the Disarmament Commission, which included Canada, France, UK, USA and USSR, had been the platform for test-ban talks from 1955. However, only at its last session held at Lancaster House in London from March to September 1957, some progress, albeit modest, was achieved. In June 1957, USSR agreed to establish an international control system which was related to an agreement on cessation of tests, including control posts on its own territory. It also proposed the suspension of tests temporarily for a two-three years period.[12] USA, UK, however, proposed a test ban only as a part of a package of 12 items embracing conventional and nuclear disarmament.[13]

According to Edmonds, while Eisenhower himself had announced in 1957 that he favoured a test ban for two reasons: the dangers posed by the fall-out and the need to curb an arms race, but it had provoked an opposition from scientists and engineers working on the American weapons programme. He established a Science Advisory Committee and put two questions to it: Would a test ban be in the interest of USA? Could compliance with such a ban be monitored adequately? The Committee answered "Yes" to both.[14] The scientists stressed the value of a test ban, not to prevent a fall-out but as a first step in controlling arms race.[15]

On 31 March 1958, the Soviet Union passed a decree stopping tests and Premier Khruschev invited the Western powers to do likewise, reserving the right of Soviet Union to resume tests if the West refused to stop. Eisenhower replied that the proposal had been made by USR after "it had completed tests of unprecedented intensity."[16] He repeated that the test ban should be part of a general disarmament agreement and proposed that a group of experts should be established to study control measures and develop a comprehensive plan for monitoring a test ban as a precondition for political talks. Khruschev, while insisting that such special studies were unnecessary, expressed his apprehensions that a technical study would delay the stopping of tests. Nevertheless, he agreed that both sides should designate experts "who would immediately begin a study of methods for detecting possible violations of an agreement on the cessation of nuclear tests."[17] USA accepted the proposal with a caveat that the agreement should not prejudice the position of two sides concerning the timing and interdependence of various aspects of disarmament. USA was thus still preserving the possibility of linking a test ban to general disarmament.

The Conference of Experts

As a result of this agreement, the Conference of Experts met in Geneva for several weeks in summer of 1958. Scientists from USA, USSR, UK, Canada, France, Czechoslovakia, Poland and Romania took part.[18] The mandate of the Conference covered negotiations for scientific aspects of monitoring nuclear explosions but not the negotiations for a test ban. This new body assured equal representation of the political groups. It was no longer in the framework of the UN but the UN provided the Secretariat and the meetings were held at the UN office in Geneva.

NUCLEAR TEST BAN

The Report of the Conference stated that workable monitoring system, to detect nuclear explosion was "technically feasible." However, the Conference recognized gaps and uncertainties in the control system which should be implemented by a network of 160-170 control posts on land and about 10 ships, each post staffed with 30 specialists, whereas collection of radioactive debris was thought to require additional provisions for on-site and aerial inspections. The report was interpreted by many observers as indicating that a nuclear test-ban was within reach. However, the factual content of final report did not support such an optimistic evaluation since the problem of verification was not entirely solved. The proposed monitoring network would not be able to detect underground explosions of yields below 5 kilotons. Neither could it detect high altitude or space detonation of about 50 kilotons. Also, the locations of the monitoring stations were not specified and the issue of underground nuclear tests was considered but not solved.[19] In the final analysis, this grotesquely elaborate verification scheme, which would have cost billion of dollars, was not only technically unweildy and politically unacceptable to many. Even from the scientific point of view it was untenable, because it was founded on the seismic expereience of "a single US test."[20] On 22 August 1958, President Eisenhowever proposed, in view of the Geneva report of Conference of Experts, that all nuclear-weapon states to meet on 31 October 1958 for negotiations on test ban and the creation of an international verification system. In addition, he proposed suspension of nuclear testing for one year, beginning with the first day of negotiations, and stated US willingness to prolong the moratorium if USSR did likewise. The Soviet Union accepted the US proposal to start negotiations but did not take a clear position on the proposed suspension of nuclear tests (it had broken off the moratorium in September 1958, conducting a series of 20 tests in the

Soviet Arctic and in Siberia). USA and UK stopped testing in time. USSR reserved the right to continue nuclear testing until it had exploded as many nuclear devices as the other two nuclear weapon states had done, but suspended nuclear testing on 3 November 1958.[21]

Towards Partial Test Ban Treaty

The First Phase

Negotiations from now on (1958) till 1963 when the Partial Test Ban Treaty was signed continued in three phases. The conference opened on 31 October 1958 in Geneva and immediately ran into difficulties. Controversies emerged on two points: (a) Name: the Soviets wanted the conference to deal with "cessation" of nuclear tests, but US stated it should deal with "suspension" of tests. In other words, the Soviets wanted a permanent ban but USA pursued a temporary ban;[22] (b) Agenda: USSR insisted that an agreement on discontinuance of nuclear tests be achieved before verification was considered. USA, however, called for the reverse. The problem was resolved in an informal meeting, when both sides agreed to a "rotating agenda" which meant that the two sides would alter the order of the agenda in a two-day rhythm.

Yet there was another controversy relating to verification. It related to verification organization and monitoring system. USA and UK advocated an international organization (internationally staffed), with decisions to be made by a majority votes. Most importantly, on-site inspections could be made whenever a questionable event occurred. USSR, on the other hand, said that it had already made a concession by accepting international monitoring based on the one outlined in the Final Report of the Conference of Experts and that it would accept only a comprehensive and permanent test ban. It expressed concerns that the proposed monitoring system could be used for intelligence purposes and therefore, supported a system under which it could "retain control of all operations on (its) own country." With respect to envisaged "control commission" USSR called for an equal number of seats for the Western and socialist groups and no more than one seat for the group of non-aligned states. It also said that the decisions be taken unanimously. Later the Soviet Union accepted the idea of an annual quota of on-site inspections.

USA thus favoured the principle of impartial verification by persons expected not to favour a principal party to the agreement. USSR insisted on principle of reciprocal verification—each party determines whether the other is living up to the agreement. USA had obtained new seismic data from the test series conducted before the conference. Accordingly, it was more difficult to differentiate earthquakes from underground nuclear explosion than had been envisaged previously. While USSR did not accept these—the basis being Geneva Conference—the US position changed, particularly regarding number of monitoring stations. Two other technical difficulties that USA brought further were: (a) detection of nuclear tests in outer space, and (b) decoupling where the test would be conducted in a large cavity so as to weaken seismic signal.[23]

In December 1959, President Eisenhower issued a statement saying that the voluntary moratorium (first announced on 26 August 1958) would expire on 31 December and that although USA considered itself free to resume testing it would not do so, "without announcing its intention in advance."[24] Meanwhile it would continue its "active programme of weapon research, development and laboratory-type experimentation." On 3 January 1960, Premier Khruschev said that the Soviet Union would not resume testing unless the West did so.

In February 1960, the West proposed a ban on nuclear tests in the atmosphere, in outer space to the height controllable, under water and underground above a seismic magnitude of 4.75.[25] Thirty per cent of all unidentified seismic events would be subject to on-site inspections. USSR, on the other hand, maintained its position that for verification of a treaty, national technical means would suffice.[26] To overcome the stalemate it proposed a moratorium on underground nuclear explosions below 4.75, while all other nuclear tests would be banned.

Despite this myriad of problems, negotiations continued in 1959-1960 with each side making concessions. Hardly had the treaty begun to take shape, the U-2 spy plane incident on 1 May 1960 dashed all hopes. Negotiations went into recess on 5 December 1960. At the 1960 UN General Assembly, USA emphasized that it had not resumed tests, although the moratorium had ended on 31 December 1960.[27] At Geneva on 26 July 1960, the Soviet Union proposed a quota of 3 on-site inspections a year.[28]

Second Phase

When negotiations were resumed in April 1961,USSR changed its position. It proposed that the control organization be headed by a troika, the test ban issue be linked to general and complete disarmament and France, which had conducted (first) nuclear test explosion in February 1961, be included in negotiations.[29] In April 1961, USA and UK submitted a draft treaty [30] which proposed twenty annual on-site inspections—eight less than originally suggested.[31] On 28 August 1961,UK and USA put forward proposals including an offer to abandon the threshold on underground nuclear explosion if the number of control posts or on-site inspections(OSI's) were increased. When Premier Khruschev met the newly elected President Kennedy in Vienna in June 1961, he proposed that either a test ban be concluded on the Soviet basis or test ban be considered in the context of general and complete disarmament so that all disarmament problems were solved together. This was similar to the position taken earlier by the United States. But the West opposed the proposal and protested that Soviet policies blocked progress on test ban. They proposed to drop the 4.75 threshold if enough control posts and OSI's were provided for.

On 30 August 1961, the Soviet Union declared that it was resuming testing. This was also the period when it faced several challenges — the pressure on Berlin, the 'Bay of Pigs' incident and the increasing US expenditure for construction of long-range missiles following the scare about 'missile gap'. The Soviets thus started extensive test series the next day.[32] Although USA and UK had indicated a willingness to agree to a ban on tests in atmosphere without international control, subsequently they two resumed testing.

In UN General Assembly in 1961, there were protests at renewed tests, provoked in particular by the Soviet announcement on 17 Otober that it was about to test a 50 megaton prototype of a 100-megaton weapon.[33] The test took place on 30 October 1961 and was estimated by US authorities at 58 megaton.

In November 1961, the Soviet Union proposed a treaty outlawing tests above ground and monitored by national technical means combined with a moratorium on underground tests until an inspection sytstem was introduced as part of general and complete disarmament. The West rejected the view put forward by the Soviet Union that inspection before general disarmament meant espionage and held that the new Soviet proposal went back on recommendations of 1958 (Conference of Experts). On 29 January 1962, the Geneva Conference on test ban adjourned *sine die*.

On 4 March 1962, the test ban issue was put on the agenda of the Eighteen Nation Committee on Disarmament (ENDC) in Geneva, which established a sub-committee for the purpose. On 9 August 1962, USA reduced their demand on on-site inspections to 12 and number of control posts to 80 and on 27 August USSR and USA submitted alternative draft treaties. One draft included a comprehensive test ban and verification measures according to the proposal of August 9,[34] and the other a partial test ban prohibiting the nuclear explosions in the atmosphere, in outer space and under water, without international verification.[35]

Third Phase

The Cuban missile crisis of October 1962, when mankind faced a holocaust of nuclear war, marked a turning- point in superpower relations and also in the test ban issue. It has been regarded by many as the progenitor of the Partial Test Ban (PTB) because it created an urgent need for a demonstrative act of reconciliation and detente. It is interesting to note that a test ban was mentioned precisely in this connection at the height of the crisis.

When the Eighteen Nations Disarmament Committee (ENDC) met in February 1963, the discussions confirmed that there was agreement on several methods of monitoring a comprehensive test ban (CTB): the use of national technical means, the use of black boxes and an annual quota of on-site inspections.

In the ENDC, USSR had proposed the use of automatic seismic stations (black boxes) to monitor compliance with a CTB and to commence discussions on the number of on-site inspections. In February 1963, USSR shifted its position considerably when it proposed two to three on-site inspections per year, the installation of three automatic stations on the territory of each nuclear power and the establishment of international commission of scientists, as proposed by eight non-aligned members of the ENDC.[36] In August 1962, the eight non-aligned members of the ENDC submitted a joint memorandum which proposed the establishment of an International Commission, comprising a limited number of highly qualified scientists possibly from the non-aligned states. This Commission was to be entrusted with the task of processing data on nuclear explosions and to report suspicious events. Any party to the treaty could invite the Commission to inspect the territory or site where the event had occurred.[37]

In the meantime, USA also changed its position and suggested seven unmanned stations and seven annual on-site inspections[38] (from the initial proposal of 28 it came down to 20 to 12 to 10 and finally to seven). In addition, attention was beginning to be turned to the modalities of on-site inspection, an issue which might have been the cause of a further round of disagreement, even if number of on-site inspections had been settled.[39]

In the wake of a somewhat optimistic climate, high level discussions took place from April to June 1963. These discussions led to the US-USSR 'hotline agreement' and to the agreement to convene a meeting on test ban issue in Moscow on 15 July 1963. On 2 July, Premier Khruschev declared that the West was asking for on-site inspections not in order to monitor the cessation of tests but in order to legalize espionage and that the Western demands for on-site inspections had made a comprehensive test ban impossible (he thus withdrew the offer of two-to-three on-site inspections). However, he said that the Soviet Union was ready to sign a PTB. Thus the negotiations of PTB without a moratorium or any other limit on underground tests were negotiated in July. The treaty was signed on 5 August 1963 in

Moscow by foreign ministers of USA, UK and USSR. It came into force on 10 October 1963.

Partial Test Ban Treaty

The treaty prohibited any nuclear weapon test explosion, or any other explosion (including peaceful nuclear explosions—PNE's) at a place under the jurisdiction or control of the Party (Article I) in the following three environments: "the atmosphere, beyond its limits, including outer space, or under water, including territorial water or high seas" (Article I, 1a). It did not prohibit nuclear underground explosions. Since no commonly agreed definition of "atmosphere" and "space" existed, the treaty applied to the area "from the surface of the earth on, into outer space" and any environment in between. [40] Although the Treaty explicitly stated that underground nuclear explosions were not subject to the Treaty, it respected environmental concerns by prohibiting nuclear explosions "in any other environment if such explosion causes radioactive debris to be present outside the territorial limits of the State under whose jursidcition or control the explosion is conducted" (I, 1b). This means that underground nuclear explosions which release radioactive debris werenot outlawed if the debris remained within the territorial limits. This meant imbalance between states with large territories and states of small size. The parties agreed to "refrain from causing, encouraging or anyway participating in, the carrying out (Article I,2) of any nuclear explosion in environments banned by the Treaty."

All states were invited to join the Treaty (Article III) which was of "unlimited duration" (Artivle IV) . Each party was given "the right to withdraw from the Treaty if... extraordinary events, related to the subject matter of that Treaty, have jeopardized the supreme interests" of the state (Article IV). Any amendment to the Treaty was to be "approved by a majority of the votes of all parties including the votes of all original parties", namely, UK, USA and USSR (Article II, 2). With this, the three nuclear-weapon states preserved the right to veto an amendment. Although Article II, 1 requires the original parties to convene a conference when one-third of the parties wish to do so, the procedures of the conference are not regulated. No provisions on verfication of compliance are contained in the Treaty. National technical means may, therefore, be used in accordance with international law. International monitoring procedures were not regarded necessary.

The PTBT may have answered or pacified the curiosities of environmental concerns but in terms of realizing its objective of curbing nuclear arms race it has proved to be a failure. In fact President Kennedy could muster the Administration's support for ratifying the treaty only after he pledged to implement a full range of safeguards. A vigorous programme of underground testing would go forward and USA would "forthwith" resume atmosphere testing if the Soviets did; facilities to detect the ban violations would be improved and USA would keep its weapon laboratories strong.

In fact, the number (and rate) of tests increased after the conclusion of the treaty and major improvements in nuclear weaponary were made, e.g., multiple independently retargettable vehicles (MIRV). The objectives sought in the preamble calling on the original parties to "achieve the discontinuance of all test explosions of all nuclear weapons for all time" and to be "determined to continue negotiations to this end," remained a dead letter. Presently 119 states are parties to the Treaty and have so far abided by the provisions. France and China are not parties to the Treaty but ceased atmospheric testing in 1975 and 1985.[41]

The next international arms control measure negotiated

was the 1968 Treaty on Non-Proliferation of Nuclear Weapons (NPT). CTBT could find a place only in the preamble where they agreed to continue neogitations on it. Under Article VI of the Treaty they agreed to the less committed obligation to "pursue negotiations in good faith on effective measures relating to cessation of nuclear race at an early date."

Test Ban Proposals during 1965-73 in Eighteen Nation Diarmament Committee(ENDC)/Conference of the Committee on Diarmament (CCD)

In 1965, Sweden submitted a paper suggesting a system of international coordination in the detection of underground nuclear explosions by an exchange of seismic data.[42] The then UAR sought prohibition on underground nuclear explosions above a seismic magnitude of 4.75 and an agreement on a moratorium on tests below this threshold.[43] For verification purposes, an exchange of data was suggested. While USA and UK rejected the proposal, citing resumption of testing by Soviet Union in 1961 as the reason, USSR stated its willingness to halt nuclear tests by establishing a moratorium.[44]

In 1966, Sweden proposed an arrangement for on-site inspections, making a distinction between mandatory inspections and inspection by challenge or invitation.[45] USSR insisted on its previous position that no international inspections were needed to verify the compliance with the treaty.[46] USA and UK stressed their belief in the necessity of such inspections.[47] USSR and USA were prepared to take part in international exchange of seismic data.[48] UK suggested limiting the annual number of underground tests which would be "phased out over a period of four to five years."[49] Japan submitted a similar proposal in 1969.[50]

In 1969, Sweden submitted a proposal reiterating its

earlier stand; a revised version of it was submitted in 1971.[51] In 1970, Canada using seismic information from 33 countries advocated establishment of an international network of siesmological stations.[52] In 1972, both Canada and Sweden submitted a paper "concerning international agreement to distinguish shallow earthquakes from underground nuclear tests."[53] In 1971, a joint memorandum of nine CCD members proposed that PTBT be complemented so as to enlarge its scope.[54] In 1972, Japan proposed a threshold of 5.25 seismic magnitude.[55] USA refused to enter into negotiations citing inadequate verifications means.[56] USSR, on the other hand, argued that a restriction on the number and size of underground nuclear tests" would not put a stop to building of nuclear arsenals."[57]

Notes and References

1. Robert A. Divine, *Blowing on the Wind: The Nuclear Test Ban Debate, 1954-1960*, Oxford University Press, New York, 1978, p.3.
2. G. Allen Greb, 'Survey of Past Nuclear Test Ban Negotiations' in Jozef Goldblat and David Cox (eds.), *Nuclear Weapon Tests: Prohibition or Limitation?*, Oxford University Press, 1988, p.96.
3. *Official Records of the Disarmament Commission*, Supplement for April, May and June, 1954, Document DC/44 and Corr 1.
4. Divine, op.cit., n.1, p.21.
5. *Official Records of the General Assembly*, Ninth Session, Plenary Meetings, 492d Meeting.
6. *Official Records of the General Assembly*, Tenth Session, Annexures Agenda item 59, Document A/2949 and Add 1; A/RES/913 (X).
7. Thomas Schmalberger,'In Pursuit of a Nuclear Test Ban Treaty: A Guide to Debate in the Conference on Disarmament',

United Nations Institute for Disarmament Research, UN, New York, 1991, p.16.
8. *Official Records of the Disarmament Commission*, Supplement for April to December 1955, Document DC/71, Annex.15, (DC/SC.1/26/Rev.2).
9. *United Nations and Disarmament*, New York: UN, 1970, p.197.
10. *Official Records of the General Assembly*, Eleventh Session, Annexures, Agenda item 22, document A/C. I/L. 162 Rev.1.
11. Robert A. Divine, op.cit., no.1, p.125.
12. *Official Records of the Disarmament Commission*, Supplement for January to December 1995, Document DC/112. Annex.12 (DC?SC.1/60).
13. Ibid., Document DC/113, Annex. 5 C BC/SC 1/66)
14. John Edmonds, 'At Last, a Total Ban on Nuclear Test ?' in J.B. Poole and R. Gutherie (eds.), *Verification 1994, Arms Control, Peacekeeping and Environment*, Brassey (UK), p.35.
15. Minutes of PSAC meetings, 8,9,10 April 1958, PSAC Records, Dwight Eisenhower Papers, cited in n.2, p.96.
16. *Geneva Conference on Discontinuance of Nuclear Weapon Tests*, Department of State Publication 7258, Washington, October 1961, p.14.
17. *Geneva Conference*, n. 16, pp 14-15, US Department of State, Documents on Disarmament, 1945-49, Vol.2, US Government Printing Office: Washington DC, 1960, p.1038.
18. United Nations, Department of Political and Security Council Affairs, *The United Nations and Disarmament: 1945-1970*, United Nations: New York, 1970, p.75.
19. Document A/4078.
20. Jozef Goldblat, 'Banning Nuclear Tests: Can CTB be Achieved?' in the *Council for Arms Control*, No.49, May 1990, p.10.
21. Document A/3985.
22. Christen Jonsson, *Soviet Bargaining Behaviours*, New York: Columbia University Press, 1979, p.26.
23. *The Test Ban: SIPRI Research Report*, Armgvist and Wilksell, 1971, p.4.
24. *Documents on Disarmament*, 1955-59. Vol. 2, US Government Printing Office : Washington DC, note 10, pp.1440-1, 1590-1.

25. At that time of its proposition, in 1965, it was assumed that a seismic magnitude of 4.75 would roughly correspond to 15 kilotons in hard rock. *SIPRI Yearbook, 1979: World Armaments*, p.456.
26. ENDC/IPV.8.
27. *The United Nations and Disarmament*, (UN, New York, 1970) p.214.
28. US Department of State, Documents on Disarmament 1961 (Deparmtment of State Publications 7172 Washington, July 1961, p.178.
29. Thomas Schmalberger, op.cit., p. 22.
30. ENDC/9, United Kingdom of Great Britain and North Ireland and United States of America, 'Draft Treaty on the Discontinuance of Nuclear Test.'
31. ENDC/PV.13.
32. G. Allen Greb and Whleckrotte, 'The Long History, The Test Ban Debate,' *Bulletin of Atomic Scientists*, August/September 1983, p.38.
33. US Arms Control and Disarmament Agency, Documents on Disarmament 1961, ACBA, Publication 5, (Washington, August 1962), p.535.
34. ENDC/58, United Kingdom/United States, 'Draft Treaty Banning Nuclear Weapons in all Environments'.
35. ENDC/59, 'Draft Treaty Banning Nuclear Weapons in the Atomosphere, in Outer Space and Underwater'.
36. ENDC/PV.101 (USSR).
37. ENDC/28, Brazil, Burma, Ethiopia, India, Mexico, Nigeria, Sweden and UAR Joint Memorandum.
38. ENDC/PV 108; ENDC/PV.110; ENDC/PV.113.
39. US Arms Control and Disarmaments Agency, Documents on Disarmament, 1963, ACDA Publication 24 (Washington, October 1964) pp.141, 182 and 205.
40. According to prevailing interpretation, this included signatories as well as "non-self governing territories administered by the state parties, and territories under military occupation." Jozef Goldblat, 'The Nuclear Explosion Limitation Treaties' in Jozef Goldblat and David Cox (eds.), *Nuclear Weapon Tests; Prohibition or Limitation?* (Oxford University Press, New York, 1968), p.121.

41. Australia and New Zealand claimed to have suffered from radioactivity which was caused by French nuclear tests in the Pacific. They brought France to International Court of Justice, which indicated that "France should avoid nuclear tests causing the deposit of radioactive fall out." (A/Res/3077, XXVIII).
42. ENDC/154 (Sweden), 'Memorandum on International Cooperation for Detection of Underground Nuclear Explosion.'
43. ENDC/PV 224-230 and 231 (UAR).
44. ENDC/PV 230, 271, 286, 402 and 409 (UAR).
45. ENDC/PV 256 (Sweden)
46. ENDC/PV 415 (UK) and ENDC/PV.209 (US).
47. ENDC/PV 286 (USSR).
48. ENDC/PV 286 (US).
49. ENDC/PV 232 (UK).
50. ENDC/PV 424 (Japan).
51. ENDC/242 (Sweden), 'Working Paper with Suggestions as to Possible Provisions of a Treaty Banning Underground Nuclear Weapon Tests.'
52. ENDC/PV 231, 332, 389 (Canada).
53. CCD/380 (Canada and Sweden), 'Working Paper on an Experiment in International Cooperation: Short Period Seismological Discrimination of Shallow Earthquakes and Underground Nuclear Explosions'.
54. CCD/354 (Burma, Egypt, Ethiopia, Mexico, Morrocco, Pakistan, Sweden and Yugoslavia), 'Joint Memorandum on Comprehensive Test Ban.'
55. CCD/PV. 553 (Japan).
56. A/C 1/PV. 1829, A/C 1/PV 1830.
57. A/C. 1/PV, 1841, A/C. 1/PV. 1847.

Chapter 2
Test Ban Negotiations Till 1980

Threshold Test Ban Treaty (TTBT)

In the beginning of seventies, the focus shifted to strategic nuclear weapons, although the test-ban issue had remained on the disarmament agenda. SALT I was "successfully" completed in 1972 but there were major roadblocks in the subsequent SALT II negotiations. At a summit meeting in July 1974, President Nixon and General Secretary Breznev signed a Threshold Test Ban Treaty (TTBT), limiting the yield of underground tests to 150 kilotons. The treaty did not come into force until 31 March 1976 and in this interval USA detonated 12 devices with a declared yield in excess of 200 kilotons. The Soviets tested five times above 200 kilotons in this period (one of which may have been a double explosion).[1] According to Schmalberger, TTBT was hastily hammered out — in only five weeks — because there was no (other) agreement ready for signing.[2]

Ratification of the TTBT was, however, postponed because USA decided it could not rely on unverified information supplied by the other side as agreed under the treaty.

In 1982 President Reagan announced that he had decided against a resumption of the CTBT negotiations, which were relegated to being only one among the USA's long-term arms control objectives. Instead, he wished to renegotiate the verification provisions of the TTBT and the Peaceful Nuclear Explosion Treaty (PNET). This was at once condemned by USSR as "no more than a pretext for sabotaging the CTB negotiations."

In the beginning of 1985, the Soviet Union declared a unilateral moratorium on nuclear testing, inviting the United States to join it and to re-open negotiations on a CTB. The United States refused both offers and continued to test. The Soviets extended their moratorium several times, but resumed testing in 1987.

In 1986, the Natural Resources Defense Council (NRDC), a private American organization, and the Soviet Academy of Sciences agreed to install temporary seismic stations on Soviet territory to monitor the moratorium. Ten-ton and 20-ton chemical explosions were detonated near the nuclear test range, from which the seismic characteristics of the local geology could be determined, which enabled improvements to be made in teleseismic yield estimation. When the Soviets resumed testing they at first required NRDC to turn off their instruments, but subsequently allowed seismic measurements of nuclear tests. In 1988 the Soviet Academy of Sciences, the US Geological Survey and the US University Consortium, Incorporated Research Institutes in Seismology (IRIS), concluded an agreement to operate seismic stations within the Soviet Union as part of the global IRIS seismic network.[3] The data from in-country seismic stations have greatly increased knowledge of local geology and experience in monitoring nuclear explosions.

The deadlock was broken only when President Gorbachev came to power in 1985. He declared that USSR was ready to resume talks on a CTBT immediately and at the same time announced a moratorium on Soviet tests. At the summit meeting in Reykjavik in 1986, he persuaded President Reagan to agree to talks on a stepwise, parallel programme of limiting and eventually ending tests. In 1987 the two countries began negotiations on additional verification provisions for the TTBT and the PNET, resulting in new protocols being signed in June 1990 and the two treaties were ratified three months later. But the relevance of this protracted exercise to the issue of nuclear testing was minimal.

From 1987 until 1990, USA and the Soviet Union were engaged in negotiations on new protocols for the TTBT and PNET. They differed on the subject of hydrodynamic yield measurement of nuclear explosions. USA sought the more instrusive on-site monitoring technique CORRTEX, whereas the Soviet Union maintained that remote seimological monitoring was sufficient. In an attempt to find common ground for a mutually acceptable method of verifying the limitation of yield, the two sides concluded a Joint Verification Experiment (JVE), to take place in 1988. Accordingly, scientists from both the countries were to be present when nuclear underground tests were conducted at Nevada test site in USA and at the Semipalatinsk test site in the Soviet Union. Hydrodynamic and teleseismic techniques were used to measure the yield of explosions which were near the 150 kilotons threshold.

An American organization, Natural Resources Defense Council (NRDC), a private US environment group, found that the bedrock at the Soviet test site was considerably harder than at Nevada test site. This explained why American seismologists had detected a higher threshold.

In spite of the improvements in seismic verification technology and the diminishing credibility attached to the accusations of Soviet violations, USA insisted upon renegotiating the protocols to the TTBT and the PNET, based on an intrusive technique for measuring explosive yield known as CORREX (Continuous Reflectometry for Radius versus Time Experiment) to be developed jointly with the Soviet Union. The Joint Verification Experiment (JVE) consisted of two explosions in 1988: at the American test site in Nevada on 17 August, and at the Soviet Semipalatinsk test site on 14 September, the data from which were fully shared by the American and the Soviet participants. The Soviet Union and the United States prepared a joint report on the JVE, but the leader of the American team was instructed not to sign it, and USA has continued to insist that the report remains classified.[4] According to a report in the *Washington Post*,[5] the yield estimate for the Nevada test site explosion was between 155 and 163 kilotons, which exceeded the treaty limit. However, Soviet seismic measurements, as reported in TASS, produced a yield estimate of 140 kilotons, in compliance with the unratified treaty limit.

On 1 June 1990, President Bush and President Gorbachev signed new protocols to the TTBT and the PNET, based on the experience gained in the Joint Verification Experiment. These protocols introduced a level of complexity unprecedented in the history of test-ban negotiations.

The Treaty (TTBT) obliges the two superpowers "to prohibit, to prevent, and not to carry out any underground nuclear weapon test having a yield exceeding 150 kilotons" (Article I,1). It was agreed to "limit the number of ... underground nuclear weapon tests to a minimum" (Article I,2) and to continue negotiations on a cessation of all nuclear weapons tests (Article I,3). The diminution of the number of tests has been interpreted by some US experts as keeping test programmes "to the minimum national security needs"[6] and not as an actual reduction of the number of tests. In Article III, the Parties agreed that the Treaty was not to apply to nuclear explosions for peaceful purposes but they committed themselves to an early resolution of the matter. As with the PTBT, each Party could withdraw from the Treaty if it perceived that its security interests were jeopardized.

The TTBT was the first test limitation agreement to include verification provisions. In addition to verification based on National Technical Means (NTM) (Article II ,1), mainly through seismic monitoring, the Treaty provided for an exchange of geological and seismological data for the calibration of yields (Protocol I,a-d). Moreover, the Treaty obliged the Parties "not to interfere with the national technical means of verification" (Article II,2), which could be interpreted as a prohibition on conducting tests in such a way as to muffle the seismic signals.[7] In addition, it was agreed that all nuclear weapons tests should be conducted solely within the testing areas reported in the data exchange. Only peaceful applications of nuclear explosions were permitted outside these areas.

The new protocol provided several additional verification measures such as on-site hydrodynamic measurement of the explosion and in-country seismic monitoring. The placement of three in-country seismic stations was agreed.[8] During a test, the verifying Party was permitted to be present at the seismic stations and to carry out seismic monitoring. The new protocol also permitted on-site inspections, including the sampling of geological material. On-site inspections were permitted if the planned yield of the explosion was to exceeed 35 kilotons (Section VII of the 1990 Protocol to the TTBT). The establishment of the Bilateral Consultative Commission (BCC) which would meet at the request of either party to discuss the implementation of, or compliance with the Treaty, as well as possible amendments to the Treaty was also agreed to (Section XI of the 1990 Protocol to the TTBT).

The new protocol to the TTBT contains as many as 107 pages, as compared to the protocol negotiated in 1974, which had only two pages.[9] The new protocol gave the right to conduct hydrodynamic CORRETEX tests and to collect regional seismic data for explosions having a declared yield greater than 50 kilotons. For explosions greater than 35 kilotons, the protocol allowed on-site inspection to confirm the detailed geology and emplacment conditions of the test. The protocol to the PNET contained similar provisions, but it also gave the right to observe the emplacement of the nuclear explosive if it had a declared yield larger than 35 kilotons.[10] In other words, the existence of a single threshold at 150 kilotons over which verification and compliance questions delayed progress on test ban negotiations for 16 years, was replaced by three threshold limits, at 150, 50 and 35 kilotons.

Tests conducted in non-standard geometries were made subject to special procedures in the protocols. For example, the verifying party had the right to demand 'reference tests' to correlate the yield estimate of the non-standard test with that of the reference tests. Interestingly, the protocol implicity recognized that seismic means were satisfactory as a yield-measurement standard, as they were employed to correlate CORRTEX measurements between the reference test and the test using a non-standard geometry.

The protocols were submitted at the end of June 1990 to the US Senate, which gave its advice and consent to ratify the Treaties in September.[11]

Peaceful Nuclear Explosions Treaty (PNET)

The major problem encountered in the TTBT negotiations was the issue of peaceful nuclear explosions.[12] Whereas USA had practically ceased conducting PNE's[13], USSR was still operating an extensive programme. To conclude the TTBT in time for the 1974 summit, the problem of PNE's was excluded and became the subject of negotiations held between October 1974 and April 1976. These talks resulted in the Peaceful Nuclear

Explosion Treaty (PNET) which was signed on 28 May 1976. However, due to the US request for additional verification provisions which were under negotiation between 1987 and 1990, the PNET and the TTBT were not ratified until 1990.

The PNET fulfilled the obligation expressed in Article III of the Threshold Test Ban Treaty (Article I,1) which committed the Parties to address the problem in PNE's. The scope of the Treaty was, therefore, closely connected with the TTBT. Both treaties were scheduled to enter into force on 31 March 1976 (Article I,2). The PNET consisted of nine articles, a protocol, an agreed statement and an additional protocol. It limited individual PNE's to 150 kilotons (Article III,2.a) and group explosions to 1.5 megatons (Article III,2.b.2), thereby limiting individual yields to 150 kilotons (Article III,2.b.1). Although the Treaty implicitly stated the right of the Parties to "carry out, participate or assist in carrying out explosions in the territory of another State at the request of such other State" (Article III, 1.b) it was specified that thee explosions should be conducted in conformity with Article V of the NPT and Article IV of its Protocol (Article VII,2).[14] It is noteworthy that the development of nuclear explosive devices was not considered to "constitute a peaceful application" (Agreed Statement, a) and was therefore subject to the TTBT.

Apart from NTM and data exchange, there was also agreement on the establishment of a Joint Consultative Commission (JCC) (Article V). Under the 1990 Protocol, the JCC could be used to facilitate the implementation of treaty provisions. Additionally, coordinating groups were to be established under the JCC for each explosion carried out as part of the verification activities under the new Protocol (Section XI of the 1990 Protocol to the PNET). Section III of the 1990 Protocol provided for on-site inspections by 'designated personnel' for any single or group explosion with a planned yield exceeding 35 kilotons. Furthermore, it was agreed that the hydrodynamic monitoring technique could be applied for explosions beyond the yield of 50 kilotons. In that case, however, the right to on-site inspections was to be forfeited (Section II of the 1990 Protocol to the PNET).

The PNET "has not increased the very limited arms control value of the TTBT."[15] It has not placed serious constraints on nuclear weapon development. Verifying a threshold treaty differs substantially from the verification required for a CTBT. Verification of a threshold treaty focusses on measuring the yield of announced nuclear test explosions and thus, on-site inspections, permitted only in designated sites, can suffice. The monitoring of a CTBT, on the other hand, requires the ability to detect and identify clandestine nuclear explosions. A CTBT, therefore, requires verification that is not restricted to specified events or areas.

The contribution of these two Treaties to the achievement of a CTB and to non-proliferation was widely regarded as negligible, above all because the threshold limit imposed no serious limitation on further development of nuclear weapons by the two superpowers. In any case, their subsequent history was peculiarly unsatisfactory. They had both been signed by President Brezhnev on the one hand, and, in sequence, by Presidents Nixon and Ford, on the other, and were then submitted, in July 1976, to the US Senate. Before much progress had been made President Carter came to office. His enthusiasm for a CTB left little interest in the two Treaties with their minor restrictions. The two governments simply announced that they would respect the 150 kilton limit and UK had no choice but to do likewise. Ratification of the Treaties was finally achieved in 1990.

Resumption of Trilateral Talks (1977-80) on CTB

In 1976, USSR put forward a draft resolution which demanded that all Nuclear-Weapons States participate in negotiations on a CTB. The resolution was adopted by majority in the UN General Assembly.[16] A draft treaty for a CTB was annexed to the resolution. USA and UK voted against the resolution because they regarded the verification procedures outlined in the proposal as insufficient. The proposed verification procedures included only NTM and a voluntary exchange of seismic data. The problem of PNE's was not addressed. The UN Security Council, where the five Nuclear Weapons States(NWS's) maintain the right of veto, was to serve as the forum to lodge complaints.[17] In another effort in February 1977, USSR expanded its previous draft treaty to include challenge inspections for suspected violations of the treaty.[18] Subsequent to this, the two superpowers agreed on an agenda for negotiations, and on the establishment of a working group to consider a CTB.

The British Prime Minister, James Callaghan, informed Presidents Carter and Brezhnev that the UK wished to take part. This was agreed to and the second series of tripartite negotiations opened in Geneva on 13 July 1977, 14 years after the first series.

It was generally recognized that there were three differences on matters of principle between Washington and London on the one hand, and Moscow on the other. First, the Soviets claimed, as in the past, that the West's verification requirements were unnecessarily elaborate and intrusive. Secondly, USA and UK had concluded that so-called 'peaceful' nuclear explosions (PNE's) must be banned as well as weapon tests, whereas by 1977 USSR had the only active PNE programme in the world and wished to continue it under the terms of the recently concluded PNET. Thirdly, the Soviet Union maintained that a CTBT should not come into force until both France and China had accepted it, although neither had any intention of doing so in the foreseeable future.

The first three months of negotiations were largely spent on these issues, culminating in important Soviet concessions. They proposed a moratorium on PNE's, which was to be an integral part of the CTBT, and they agreed that the treaty's entry into force need not wait for the adherence of France and China. They stipulated that both questions should be reviewed after the treaty had been in force for three years. Both USA and UK agreed.

Preliminary meetings on a CTB with the participation of UK began in July, and opened formally in October 1977.[19] The negotiations focussed on the issue of PNE's, verification, and on the desired participation of the two Nuclear-Weapon States, namely, France and China, which had not yet been parties to any test ban agreement.[20] In November 1977, USSR proposed a three-year moratorium on PNE's with provisions for possible extension. The moratorium was intended as an interregnum during which methods of distinguishing military from peaceful nuclear explosions would be explored. The Soviet Union also conceded that France and China need not be parties to a treaty for a three-year period. The Soviet Union argued, however, that for a permanent treaty it would be indispensable to include all the Nuclear-Weapon States. USA on its part, conceded that voluntary on-site inspections would be as much of a deterrent as mandatory on-site inspections. In early 1978, USSR declared its willingness to accept "black boxes" on its territory—unmanned seismic stations placed on the territory of Nuclear-Weapon States, which transmit seismic data to stations outside the country , and to agree to on-site inspections with the right of refusal. USSR was also willing to participate in research concerning the possibility of an international seismic monitoring system and to make available five of its own stations. At the same time, USA acknowledged that not all requests for inspections could be binding.

Early 1978 brought important moves on the more complex verification issue. The Soviet side accepted that any party to the treaty could ask for an on-site inspection on the territory of any other party as one way of verifying that a 'seismic event' had not been nuclear in origin; in return, USA and UK accepted that it would not be 'mandatory' for the state where the supposed event had occurred to agree to every request for an inspection. It was also agreed that two or more parties could arrange special verification measures between themselves. For the three negotiating powers, these arrangements would include detailed procedures for on-site inspections and for 'high quality national seismic stations'(NSS) to be installed on one another's territory, as set out in a separate tripartite verification agreement.

Opposition to test-ban treaty in USA was led by the nuclear-weapons laboratories, who argued that nuclear testing was essential to improve the safety and security of nuclear-weapons designs, and to maintain a reliable nuclear deterrent. The weapons scientists went on to argue that the Soviets could cheat under a CTB, gaining some military advantage.[21] Although President Carter was not persuaded by the technical necessity for a nuclear testing programme, nor dissuaded from seeking a CTB because of verification concerns, he realized that ratification of a CTB would be difficult if the directors of the laboratories were to testify against it in the Senate. Carter decided to give priority to ratifying the second Strategic Arms Limitation Treaty, and the negotiators in Geneva got bogged down in details. An important change in the American and British position concerned the treaty's duration. Early in 1978 the directors of the American nuclear-weapons laboratories, with support from their British counterparts, asserted that the reliability and hence the safety of stockpiled weapons needed periodic confirmation by carrying out tests. The two countries accordingly proposed in June 1978 that the treaty should have an initial life of five years, leaving open the options after that, including possible extension for further periods. USSR accepted this, although it expressed no need to test its own weapons for reliability or safety. Shortly afterwards USA presented proposals for 15 NSS to be sited at specified locations in the Soviet Union.

Obstruction and Frustration

In retrospect, August 1978 probably marked the high point of the negotiations. All the traditional matters of contention had been resolved, and largely in ways favoured by the West. Virtually all the articles of a CTBT and the protocol for a concurrent moratorium on PNE's had been drafted; most of the outstanding matters concerned the separate verification agreement. The three delegations expected to finish their work by early 1979.

However, this prospect caused the CTBT's opponents to intensify their efforts. Obviously inspired stories in the American press claimed that many Congressmen and Administration officials wanted the treaty's duration to be restricted to only three years, with the expectation that USA would be free to resume testing thereafter. Officials opposed to a long-term treaty appeared before the House Armed Services Committee in a public demonstration of the Administration's division on the matter. Eventually President Carter decided to go for a three-year agreement, later described by the same Committee as "the worst of both the political and military worlds." It undermined the position of Paul Warnke, the chief American negotiator for both the CTBT and SALT. It was left to his deputy to convey the decision formally to his Soviet counterpart.

TEST BAN NEGOTIATIONS TILL 1980

The eventual Soviet response was to agree, without enthusiasm, to continue negotiations on that basis and, predictably, to insist that the complex verification arrangements proposed by the Americans would be inappropriate for only a three-year period. Paul Warnke resigned in October, to the disquiet of the Soviet delegation.

Meanwhile, USA reduced its requirement for NSS in USSR from 15 to 10. After an interval, USSR accepted this number, but on the condition that USA and UK each accepted ten NSS at specified locations; nine of the British quota were to be in the dependent territories, ranging from Hongkong to the Falkland Islands. The *reductio ad absurdum* of the NSS concept was a tactically clever move which distracted the West for the remaining two years of the talks.

In January 1979, Herbert York became the new leader of the US delegation. He had long been a supporter of a CTBT; however, by the time he arrived the prospects for a successful conclusion were much reduced and, furthermore, the negotiations were increasingly affected by outside events. In Britain the Callaghan Labour government was replaced by a new Conservative administration under Margaret Thatcher. There were signs that the US Senate would not consent to the ratification of the SALT II Treaty, let alone a CTBT. And in December 1979 the Soviet invasion of Afghanistan brought East-West relations to their lowest point for several years.

The CTB negotiations continued until one week after Ronald Reagan won the 1980 Presidential elections in November, when they were 'suspended' at the request of USA.[22]

According to Herbert York, who became the chief negotiator for the United States in 1979, the most difficult issue to resolve was over the number and locations of national seismic stations on British territory.[23]

Another obstacle emerged when the US delegation requested that the seismographs for the monitoring system be manufactured in USA. Despite these obstacles, the three delegations presented a report to the CD in July 1980,[24] which represented the framework of a "potential treaty".[25]

Progress in neogitations began to slow down in 1978 when USA requested for additional seismic data and suggested that ten national seismic stations be established in USA and USSR respectively, using improved equipment and foreign personnel to install and service the stations. USA furthermore proposed to temporarily limit a CTBT to five years and finally to three years. Renewal of the treaty was to be subject to re-ratification, and very low-yield nuclear explosions were to be allowed.[26] SIPRI Yearbook 1982 has summarized the points of agreements and disagreements of these three years (1977-1980).[27]

Main Points of Agreement

UK, USA and USSR agreed that: (a) a comprehensive test ban treaty should prohibit any nuclear weapon test explosion in any environment and be accompanied by a protocol on nuclear explosions for peaceful purposes, which would establish a moratorium on such explosions; (b) any amendment to the treaty would require the approval of a majority of parties, which majority should include all parties that are permanent members of the UN Security Council, and a conference would be held at an appropriate time to review the operation of the treaty; (c) the parties would use national technical means of verification at their disposal to verify compliance and would undertake not to interfere with such means of verification; an international exchange of seismic data would be established; and (d) the treaty would provide for consultations to resolve questions that might arise concerning compliance and any party would have the right to request an on-site inspection for the purpose of ascertaining whether or not an event on the territory of another party was a nuclear explosion.

Main Points of Disagreement

Verification: While verification no longer seemed to be a major obstacle, a series of complex technical problems related to verification remained to be solved. Whatever additional methods might be used, seismological means of verification would certainly constitute the principal component of an international control system for an underground test ban. With this in mind, the Geneva-based Committee on Disarmament established an *ad hoc* group of scientific experts to consider international co-operative measures to detect and identify seismic events. The group suggested that these measures should include a systematic improvement of procedures at seismological observatories around the globe, an international exchange of seismic data and the processing of the data at special international data centres.

In particular, this group of experts considered that a seismological verification system should comprise about 50 globally distributed teleseismic stations selected in accordance with seismological requirements. These would be national facilities operated in accordance with generally accepted rules. The seismograph stations belonging to the system would routinely report the parameters of detected seismic signals, as well as transmit data in response to requests for additional information regarding events of particular interest. International centres would receive the data mentioned above, apply agreed analysis procedures to these data in order to estimate location, magnitude and depth of seismic events, associate identification paramters with these events, distribute compilations of the complete results of these analyses, and act as a data bank.[28]

Although the global seismic network could provide a high degree of assurance that a comprehensive test ban was not being violated, there might still be events of uncertain origin. One way to reduce this uncertainty, which in most cases would be related to earthquake areas, could be for the state in question to provide seismic data for the suspected event from local stations not belonging to the global network.

UK, USA and USSR agreed to develop measures of reciprocal verification, independent of the envisaged international co-operative measures, in order to obtain supplemental seismic data from high-quality, tamper-proof national seismic stations (NSS's) of agreed characteristics. Ten NSS's would be installed on the territories of USA and of USSR, but no agreement could be reached regarding the number of such stations in UK. Questions regarding the specific locations of the NSS's, their emplacement and maintenance as well as the transmission of data produced by them had not been settled.

While the three negotiating powers agreed on the possibility of having on-site inspections, the procedure for setting in motion the inspection process (including the nature of the evidence needed to justify a request for on-site inspection), the modalities of the inspection itself (including the equipment to be used), as well as the number, rights and functions of the inspectors, were yet to be specified.

Other unresolved issues: Among other issues which remained to be settled was the status of laboratory tests which could, for example, consist of extremely low-yield nuclear experiments or the so-called inertial confinement fusion.[29]

Extremely low-yield nuclear experiments could involve an explosion of a device which may have the same characteristics as a nuclear explosive device but which uses fissile material of an amount or kind that produces only a fraction of the yield of the chemical explosion that sets off the release of the nuclear energy. The question was whether such a test, which could be conducted in a laboratory, should be considered a nuclear-weapon test explosion. The inertial confinement concept is to use lasers or other high power sources to heat and compress small pellets containing fusionable fuel (deuterium and tritium). If a properly shaped pulse of sufficient energy can be delivered to the pellet, the density and temperature may become high enough for fusion. This would be a laboratory nuclear explosion of tiny proportions.

It may be argued that, in order to be effective, a comprehensive test ban should cover all explosions without exception, including laboratory tests. On the other hand, it can be contended that a comprehensive test ban could not cover laboratory tests because they are contained and not verifiable, and also because some of them may be useful for various peaceful purposes, including the development of new sources of energy.

Yet another point at issue was the duration of a comprehensive test ban treaty. The treaty negotiated trilaterally was planned to have a duration of no more than three years. USA did not want to make a provision for a possible extension of the ban, while USSR preferred to stipulate that the ban would continue unless the other nucler weapon powers, not party to the treaty, continued testing. A ban of fixed duration would not fulfil the pledge included in the PTBT to achieve the discontinuance of all test explosions of nuclear weapons for all time. Moreover, a treaty of short duration would create a problem with respect to the adherence of non-nuclear weapon states, particularly parties to the NPT, which had renounced the possession of nuclear explosive devices for a much longer period. Finally, resumption of tests upon the expiration of a short-lived comprehensive test ban treaty would probably hurt the cause of arms limitation and disarmament more than if the treaty had never been entered into.

After the submission of the Tripartite Report, the negotiations came to a standstill for more than a year. In the meantime, the American position changed significantly. A comprehensive test ban was only "an element in the full range of long-term United States arms control objectives."[30] USSR, on the other hand, stated that its position remained unchanged.[31] On 20 July 1982, USA formally ended the tripartite talks by announcing that it would not resume the negotiations.

The Reagan Administration suspended American policy to seek a CTB in 1982 in favour of moves to develop a more satisfactory verification regime for the TTBT and the PNET. USA accused the Soviet Union of 'likely violations' of the 150-kiloton limit, which became a matter of some controversy. At the heart of this controversy lay the methodology for estimating the yield of Soviet nuclear tests by teleseismic means, which was difficult to resolve, given the lack of data on the local geology of Soviet test sites.

This time opposition to American administration policy emerged from the independent scientific community. It was claimed that testing for safety, security and reliability could be done adequately with non-nuclear means. The only purpose for which nuclear testing was truly essential was to develop new types of nuclear weapons, which was precisely what a test ban was intended to prevent.[32]

Notes and References

1. Josephine Ann Spin, 'Progress Towards a Comprehensive Nuclear Test Ban', *Verification Report*, 1991, Apex Press,1991, p.46.
2. Thomas Schmalberger, 'In Pursuit of a Nuclear Test Ban Treaty : A Guide to Debate in the Conference on Disarmament', United Nations Institute for Disarmament Research, New York, 1991, p. 29.
3. G van der Vink, 'Testimony before the US Senate Select Committee on Intelligence, 10 August 1990.
4. W.K.H. Panofsky, 'Testimony before the US Senate Foreign Relations Committee', 31 July 1990.
5. R.J. Smith, 'Data from atom blast adds to treaty verification questions', *Washington Post*, 8 September 1988.
6. Jozef Goldblat, *The Nuclear Explosion Limitation Treaties*, p.129; In fact, the number of tests did not decrease.
7. Ibid, p. 130.
8. The location of these designated stations are: Tulsa/Oklahoma, Black Hills/South Dakota and Newport/Washington in US and Arti, Novosibirsk and Obninsk in USSR.
9. Protocol to the Treaty between USA and USSR on the Limitation of Underground Nuclear Weapon Tests, 1 June 1990.
10. R.F. Lehmann, 'Testimony before the US Senate Foreign Relations Committee', 17 July 1990.
11. Friends Committee on National Legislation, *Washington Newsletter*, October 1990.
12. G. Allen Greb and Warren Heckrotte, *The Long History: The Test Ban Debate*, 1988, p.39.
13. The last U.S. test in the Plowshare Program was conducted in 1973. The Program was officially terminated in 1977.
14. Article V of the NPT demands that "potential benefits from any peaceful applications of nuclear explosions will be made available to non-nuclear weapon States Party to the Treaty". This was intended to diminish inequality of the parties under the NPT. So far, only Egypt has requested assistance in the study of PNE's for building a canal through its desert region. There has been no follow-up.
15. Jozef Goldblat, *The Nuclear Explosion Limitation Treaties*, 1988, p.137.

16. A/RES/3478 (XXX).
17. A/C.1/31/9.
18. CCD/523, (Union of Soviet Socialist Republics), 'Draft Treaty on the Complete and General Prohibition of Nuclear Weapon Tests'.
19. April Carter, *Success and Failure of Arms Control Negotiations*, SIPRI. Oxford : Oxford University, 1989, p.86.
20. From the Soviet perspective China and France had to be included in a CTB for three reasons: Nuclear test explosions would have to be banned globally; China was at that time a hostile neighbour to USSR and could have continued testing; and France could be suspected of conducting proxy tests for USA (ibid p.87).
21. J.A. Stein & F.von Hippel, 'Laboratories vs a nuclear ban', *New York Times*, 28 March 1986. Stein, 'Testimony before the California Senate Committee on Health and Human Services', 11 February 1987.
22. John Edmonds. 'At last, a total ban on nuclear test', in *JB Poole and R Gutherie* (eds.), *Verification, Arms Control, Peace Making and Environment*, London, 1994, pp.37-39.
23. H. York, *Making Weapons, Talking Peace*, Basic Books, New York, 1987.
24. CD/130,)United Kingdom, United States of America and Union of Soviet Socialist Republics), "Tripartite Report in the Committee on Disarmament".
25. April Carter, *Success and Failure of Arms Control Negotiations*, op.cit., p. 89.
26. Ibid., p. 88.
27. *SIPRI Year Book 1988: World Armaments and Disarmament*, Taylor and Francis, 1982, pp.432-434.
28. Conference of the Committee on Disarmament document CCD/558, 9 March 1978.
29. 'Comprehensive Nuclea Test Ban',, Report of the UN Secretary-General, Committee on Disarmament document CD/86, 16 April 1980, pp.38-39.
30. CD/PV.152 (United States).
31. CD/PV.156(USSR).
32. J.A. Stein, 'Nuclear tests mean new weapons', *Bulletin of the Atomic Scientists*, November 1986; S. Fetter, *Toward a Comprehensive Test Ban*, Ballinger, Cambridge, 1988.

Chapter 3
The Second Cold War

Debates in UN General Assembly

In the 1978 Final Document, the General Assembly identified the cessation of nuclear-weapon tests as the most important initial measure in working towards the highest priority requirement of nuclear disarmament.[1] In 1982 and 1983 the negotiating body established an *ad hoc* subsidiary body on a test ban with a limited mandate to examine verification and control questions, but not actually to negotiate a treaty. It made no tangible progress, however, because of disagreement over that mandate. For the same reason, since 1984 the Conference had been unable to agree to set up such an ad hoc committee although it continued to have before it draft mandates from its three major groups, some of which had been revised from time to time. Basically, the Socialist States and the Group of 21 in the Conference held the view that all questions relating to verification had been adequately studied and that the actual negotiation of a treaty should be undertaken. In the opinion of most Western members, however, consideration of those questions was far from exhausted and, moreover, the question of scope—for instance, the question whether there could be peaceful nuclear explosions once a comprehensive test ban had been concluded —

also had to be examined and some understandings reached before actual negotiations could begin. In 1987 the Soviet Union, together with other Socialist States, submitted to the Conference a paper entitled 'Basic provisions of a treaty on the complete and general prohibition of nuclear-weapon tests', amplifying the verification provisions of an earlier initiative in the General Assembly.[2]

The Soviet Union attempted to break the persistent pattern of testing when, beginning on 6 August 1985, it unilaterally halted all of its nuclear explosive testing until 1 January 1986 and called upon the United States to do so as well. The Soviet moratorium, subsequently renewed a number of times, was eventually maintained for a period totalling 18 months. The United States, together with some other countries, did not accept an unverified, unilateral, revocable moratorium as a constructive initiative. It began to emphasize, however, the need for more precise means of verifying and measuring limitations on permitted tests, with a view to reaching agreement on more stringent limitations. Since relinquishing its voluntary moratorium, the Soviet Union and other East European countries as well stressed the importance of exploring all avenues in working to achieve a comprehensive test ban as early as possible.

The debates in the General Assembly continued to reflect disagreement regarding the best means of achieving the test-ban objective. Most resolutions called for action on the part of the Geneva body; others, since 1985, dealt with the possibility of converting the Partial Test Ban Treaty(PTBT) into a comprehensive instrument and, since 1986, with notifying all States, through the United Nations, of nuclear tests carried out. In 1986, the States of the Five-Continent Peace Initiative circulated in the General Assembly a document on verification measures,[3] in which they declared their readiness to co-operate with USSR and USA in monitoring a nuclear-test moratorium.

Bilateral Talks between USA and USSR

In 1986, the two major powers opened bilateral talks on verification and measurement methodology related to nuclear testing, and in November 1987 they began formal negotiations designed to lead eventually to the cessation of such testing. They agreed to conduct those negotiations on a stage-by-stage basis, with the aim of reaching, in the first stage, agreement on verification measures to make possible the ratification of the 1974 and 1976 test-limitation treaties. Thereafter, they would proceed to negotiate further intermediate limitations on nuclear testing, leading to the ultimate objective of its complete cessation as part of an effective disarmament process.[4]

Through 1988 the bilateral negotiations proceeded apace, and in the context of that effort the two parties conducted joint verification experiments on each other's territory to compare yield measurements of actual explosions, each using its own preferred measurement technology. Also in 1988, the concept of reporting to the United Nations on nuclear-test explosions and consolidating the information into an annual register was carried a step further with the announcement by France that it would henceforth report on its own tests.

No corresponding advance occurred in 1988 in the Conference on Disarmament. A new draft mandate for an *ad hoc* committee on the item submitted by the Group of 21 was rejected by the Western members of the Conference on the ground that it would be open to diverse interpretations. A compromise text proposed later by Czechoslovakia generated fresh interest, with the Socialist and Western members and some members of the Group of 21 regarding it as a possible step towards breaking the deadlock.

The two traditional General Assembly resolutions in 1988, one initiated by the non-aligned States, urging the Conference on Disarmament to undertake the negotiation of a comprehensive treaty, and the other, by Australia in conjunction with New Zealand, urging the Conference to initiate substantive work on all aspects of a treaty including its monitoring, were both adopted by large majorities. A number of States, however, maintained their positions, as indicated by negative votes, abstentions and explanations of vote. The effort to have the Partial Test Ban Treaty converted into a comprehensive instrument through an amendment conference gained further momentum with the formal submission of the proposal to the three depositary Governments by a number of parties and the adoption of another General Assembly resolution on the subject of such a conference.

In the beginning of 1989, it was reported that the Soviet Union and the United States negotiators had agreed, in their bilateral talks, on the text for the required protocol to the peaceful nuclear explosions treaty (PNET), and were moving along well with the protocol to the threshold test-ban Treaty (TTBT). The basic positions of the nuclear-weapon States during 1989 remianed essentially as they had been for a number of years.

The United States continued to view a comprehensive test ban as a long-term objective, to be achieved in the context of international security under conditions of deep and verifiable arms reductions, an appropriate balance of conventional forces, well-established greater confidence, and non-reliance on nuclear deterrent. Notwithstanding this position, it would continue its negotiations on a stage-by-stage basis with USSR, participate in multilateral work in the Conference on

Disarmament on nuclear testing under a non-negotiating mandate, and willingly fulfil its responsibilities as a depository of the Partial Test Ban Treaty with regard to the proposed amendment Conference. The United Kingdom maintained a similar view, observing that security would depend, in part, on a nuclear deterrent for the foreseeable future. It welcomed the ongoing work at the bilateral level, and believed that further steps would have to be considered following ratification of the Threshold Test Ban Treaty and Peaceful Nuclear Explosions Treaty. It, too, emphasized that it intended to carry out fully its responsibilities as a depositary of the Partial Test Ban Treaty.

The Soviet Union stressed again its willingness to explore any avenue that could lead to the early conclusion of a comprehensive test ban, including the ongoing bilateral approach, multilateral consideration of the question in a working body of the Conference on Disarmament, and the extension of the Partial Test Ban Treaty, of which it was a depositary, to cover underground explosive testing. On a reciprocal basis with the United States, moreover, it would at any time re-introduce a moratorium on all nuclear explosions. It hoped for an early conclusion of the first phase of the bilateral negotiations and, upon the ratification of the two Treaties concerned, for the immediate start of negotiations towards further intermediate limitations on nuclear testing.

China, one of the two Nuclear-Weapon States not party to the Partial Test Ban Treaty, continued to hold that the major nuclear-weapons States must take the lead in halting the development, production and deployment of nuclear weapons and in nuclear disarmament. As always, it stood for total prohibition and destruction of nuclear weapons, including the cessation of nuclear testing, and would take appropriate measures in the context of a nuclear disarmament process. It was flexible as to a mandate for a multilateral working body within the Conference on Disarmament, and would participate in its work, a position it had adopted in 1986. France, for its part, maintained that commitments regarding nuclear testing must be considered only in the context of nuclear disarmament and that the cessation of testing should not be a pre-condition, but rather the end-point of that process; thus, for it, the cessation of nuclear testing was not a valid priority in nuclear disarmament. Under current conditions it would not agree to allowing its limited nuclear deterrent to become obsolete. Already it only carried out nuclear-test explosions sufficient to maintain the credibility of that deterrent and, if there were deep reductions, the assured reliability of its remaining nuclear weapons would become more important. While it would not stand in the way of any procedural arrangement agreed to in the Conference on Disarmament, it would not participate in the work the objective of which was the negotiation of an agreement to which it could not subscribe.

The approach initiated in 1985 by Mexico and subsequently promoted also by Indonesia, Peru, Sri Lanka, Venezuela and Yugoslavia, by which a conference of the parties to the Partial Test Ban Treaty would be convened to consider amendments to the Treaty to make it include underground nuclear tests in addition to those already prohibited, continued to gain support, or at least acceptance. By early April 1985[5] forty States parties to the Treaty—more than one-third of the total—had formally requested for the convening of such a conference, in accordance with article II of the Treaty,[6] to consider and, it was hoped, to approve the proposed amendment.

Details of Negotiations[6a]

Search for a Mandate for an Ad Hoc Committee

The controversy over a time-frame in which a comprehensive test ban treaty should be negotiated was reflected in the search for a mandate for an ad hoc committee. The Conference on Disarmament can establish ad hoc committees if it deems it advisable for the effective performance of its functions, or when it appears that a basis exists to negotiate a draft treaty or other draft texts.[7]

The establishment of an ad hoc committee in the CD requires consensus.[8] During the past decade several draft mandates for an ad-hoc committee on a nuclear-test ban have been submitted to the CD. Some have called for discussions, others for the negotiation of a treaty. None have found consensus. In order to overcome the stalemate, compromise mandates were tabled. They enabled the CD to establish a subsidiary body on the test ban issue in 1982, 1983, 1990 and 1991.

Negotiating Mandates

Negotiating mandates were proposed by the Group of 21, the Group of Socialist States, and various other States. When it came to the question of finding consensus on a proposed mandate, the two political groups declared several times that they endorsed the draft mandate put forward by the other group.[9] The proposed mandates coincided in their main objective, to negotiate a test ban treaty, but differed in the way these negotiations were to be conducted. Several general drafts called only for multilated negotions of a treaty on the prohibition of all nuclear weapons tests without specifying the conduct of the negotiations. They were submitted by the G-21 in 1984, 1985 and 1986,[10] and by the Group of Socialist States in 1984 and 1985,[11] the

German Democratic Republic in 1982[12] and Mexico in 1984.[13]

Other draft mandates set forth a specific structure of the negotiations to be held. In 1985, Bulgaria and the German Democratic Republic tabled a draft that provided for negotiations on the scope of a treaty, the main obligations of States parties, the implementation, and other provisions such as entry into force and amendments.[14] A draft mandate, first proposed by Mexico in 1986 [15] and subsequently taken up by a group of member States of the CD in 1987 [16] and the Group of 21 in 1988,[17] provided for the conduct of negotiations in two working groups—one dealing with content and scope of the treaty, the other with verification and compliance.

Still other mandates were tabled while test ban negotiations were taking place outside the CD.[18] In 1981, the Group of 21 and the Group of Socialist States submitted drafts mandate while the tripartite negotiations were formally still going on. The draft of the G-21 contained the demand for parallel negotiations in the CD.[19] The proposal of the Group of Socialist States merely called for the consideration of the problem of nuclear-weapon tests in all its aspects with a view to rapidly concluding a treaty on the general and complete prohibition of nuclear weapons tests.[20]

Non-Negotiating Mandates

A non-negotiating mandate for an ad hoc committee was proposed in 1984, by the Western group without France.[21] The draft mandate called for discussions on specific issues relating to a comprehensive test ban, including scope, verification, and compliance, with a view to negotiating a treaty.[22] The mandate also requested for the examination of institutional and administrative arrangements for an internatinal seismic monitoring system.

The draft mandate was rejected by most States of the other political groups. Pakistan, however, believed that discussions under less than ideal conditions might be better than no discussion at all.[23] This view was welcomed by Sri Lanka and Sweden.[24] A similar position had already been taken earlier by Australia. It had repeatedly declared that it would welcome a full negotiating mandate but due to the absence of the consensus it was in favour of a mandate which would enable the Conference to carry out the work required for a treaty.[25]

In 1985, the same group of Western States proposed a draft programme of work for an ad hoc committee.[26] This attempt could be seen as an attempt to clarify the purpose of the proposed non-negotiating mandate because the programme of work merely sought to organize the work of an ad hoc committee, whereas the establishment of an ad hoc committee required a mandate. The proposed programme of work was divided into three major areas: scope, verification and compliance.

The scope of the envisaged treaty would ban all nuclear explosions in all environments and would include PNE's. The section on verification outlined items for discussions and comprised, among other points, National Technical Means(NTM), capabilities and improvements of an international exchange of seismic data, an international exchange of data on airborne radioactivity, and on-site inspections. Under 'compliance', the programme envisaged discussions on procedures for consultations and complaints, and institutional aspects of a Consultative Committee and a Committee of Experts. Proposals for non-negotiating mandates which aimed at a compromise led to the establishment of ad hoc committees in 1982, 1983, 1990, and 1991.

In 1982, in informal consultations conducted by the Chairperson of the Committee on Disarmament, agreement was reached on the establishment of a drafting group to formulate the mandate of a possible subsidiary body.[27] Within the drafting group, the differing positions over the negotiating character of the ad hoc committee diverted and deadlocked the discussion. Mexico, however, submitted a compromise mandate which was finally adopted. This mandate served for the ad hoc committees in 1982 and in 1983.[28] The relevant part of the mandate was:

> "Considering that discussion of specific issues in the first instance may facilitate progress towards negotiation of a nuclear test ban, the Committee requests the ad-hoc working group to discuss and define, through substantive examination, issues relating to verification and compliance with a view to making further progress towards a nuclear test ban."[29]

Although all States had accepted the mandate, its limited scope caused dissatisfaction among many.[30] They reiterated their initial rationale for their agreement on a non-negotiating mandate and stated that they had seen this mandate as the only possibility to start the negotiating process.[31] They were not willing to continue the work in the ad hoc committee without a negotiating mandate. To this end, some countries expressed their desire to broaden the mandate so as to commence negotiations on a nuclear test ban treaty without further delay.[32] They were supported by the Chairperson of the ad hoc working group in 1982 and 1983.[33] Since positions on a mandate remained inflexible, the CD was not able to establish an ad hoc committee until 1990.

Ad Hoc Committees in 1982 and 1983

The results of the work of the ad hoc Committees in 1982 and 1983 were limited. The different approaches to a nuclear test ban treaty precluded the question of a mandate and also affected the issues of scope, verification and compliance.

The ad hoc Committee of 1982 was not able to agree

on a programme of work because of two conflicting approaches. One required an agreement on the scope of a treaty before discussing verification procedures, the other called for the elaboration of verification measures "on the basis of certain broad assumptions." [34] The consequence of the former approach would have been that even though a test ban treaty would not have been negotiated, it would still have been discussed. Besides, it was argued that the consideration of the scope was not particularly mentioned in the mandate as a specific issue to be examined. The latter approach would have side-stepped any discussion of a treaty and would have focussed abstractly on verification and compliance procedures. This approach reflected the gradual step-by-step approach and was outlined in a programme of work proposed by the Netherlands. The proposal presupposed a "comprehensive and world-wide" [35] scope for a treaty, and focussed on consideration of the establishment and institutional aspects of an international monitoring system.

The ad hoc Committee of 1983 agreed on a compromise programme of work. The relevant part of the programme of work was:

> In discharging its mandate, the Ad-Hoc Group on a Nuclear Test Ban will examine issues of verification and of compliance with a NTB with a view to making further progress towards a corresponding treaty which would be non-discriminatory and could attract the widest possible adherence.

The programme envisaged a general discussion on the subject matter followed by considerations of six items comprising of: 1. Requirements and elements of verification; 2. Means of verification, *inter alia* (a) national technical means and (b) international exchange of seismic data; 3. Procedures and mechanisms for consultation and cooperation; 4. The Committee of Experts;

5. Procedures for complaints; and, 6. On-site inspection. This portion of the programme of work satisfied the requirement to discuss verification and compliance whereas the following statement included in the programme of work offered the possibility of extending the discussions.

"In the examination of issues relating to verification and compliance consideration should be given to all relevant aspects of a treaty on a Nuclear Test Ban."

Details of Trends

During informal consultations at the beginning of 1987 session, Ambassador Vejvoda of Czechoslovakia submitted an informal draft mandate. Although it could not be adequately addressed in that session, in the next session of CD in 1988, it was submitted as draft mandate by Czechoslovakia (CD/863, Czechoslovakia). By July 1990, most countries agreed on the mandate which led to its adoption. France restated that it was not willing to participate in an ad hoc committee on test ban in the framework of CD. China participated for the first time.

The relevant part of the mandate, namely, paragraphs 2 through 4, which also served as the *de facto* programme of work, read:

"The Conference requests the Ad-Hoc Committee to initiate as a first step towards achieving a nuclear test ban treaty, substantive work on specific and interrelated test ban issues, including structure and scope as well as verification and compliance.

"Pursuant to its mandate, the Ad-Hoc committee will take into account all existing proposals and future initiatives. In addition, it will draw on the knowledge and experience that have been accumulated over the years in the consideration of a comprehensive test ban in the successive multilateral negotiating bodies and the trilateral negotiations.

"The Conference also requests the Ad-Hoc Committee to examine the institutional and administrative arrangements necessary for establishing, testing and operating an international seismic monitoring network as part of an effective verification system of a nuclear test ban treaty. The Ad-Hoc Committee will also take into account the work of the Ad-Hoc Group of Scientific Experts to Consider International Cooperative Measures to Detect and Identify Seismic Events."

The novelty of this mandate was the introduction of the term "structure" which was not defined but could be interpreted as the structure of a nuclear test ban treaty. Countries that were opposed to a negotiating mandate for an ad hoc committee on a nuclear test ban, regarded their acceptance of the word "structure" as a concession to those States which preferred a negotiating mandate. The reason for this concession might have been the interest in the establishment of an ad hoc committee to provide a sign of goodwill before the Fourth NPT Review Conference and the Amendment Conference. The NPT Review Conference put pressure on USA and UK because some countries had indicated that they would link the adoption of a final document from the Review Conference, to a commitment by the nuclear-weapons powers to conclude a CTBT within five years. The Amendment Conference aimed to amend the PTBT in such a way as to convert the PTBT into a CTBT, an approach that USA and UK rejected. It soon became evident that the term "structure" had been acceptable to USA and UK because of its ambiguity which permitted them to interpret the new mandate in a similar vein as the previous compromise mandates. Those countries favouring a negotiating mandate, however, interpreted the word "structure" as a reference to discussions of a treaty. The ensuing controversy paralyzed, to a large extent, the work of the 1990 ad hoc Committee.

Discussions on Scope

Discussions on the scope of a nuclear test ban treaty focussed on two issues: the inclusion of PNE's in a test-ban agreement, and the requested participation of all declared nuclear weapons states for the entry into force of a nuclear test ban treaty.

Peaceful Nuclear Explosions(PNE's)

In 1974, USA and USSR agreed on the TTBT which limited only the yield of nuclear-weapon tests, and excluded nuclear explosions for peaceful purposes from its scope. Although the same yield limitation was applied to PNE's in the PNET, signed in 1976, the differentiation was formally manifested in these agreements. Thereafter, the two superpowers declared that this distinction was artificial becuase PNE's could not be distinguished from nuclear weapons tests. Some states, however, insisted on this distinction because they felt that the peaceful application of nuclear explosions might be valuable for their economic development. If PNE's provide potential benefits, the NPT permits non-nuclear weapons States to use them, but requires that the PNE devices be provided by nuclear-weapons states. Presently, however, the nuclear-weapons States are not known to have active PNE programmes, and none of the non-nuclear weapons state has asked for assistance. In the Conference on Disarmament three views emerged from the discussion on the issue of PNE's.

(a) One view considered that a comprehensive test ban treaty should cover all nuclear explosions without any distinction between nuclear weapons tests and the peaceful application of nuclear explosions.[36] In 1983, the United Kingdom introduced a paper which pointed to the problems that PNE's would cause for a nuclear test ban treaty. It stated that the basic technologies for nuclear weapons and peaceful nuclear explosives were identical and, therefore, any nuclear explosive could be used as a weapon. Seismic recordings would show no distinction. The only difference would be in the declared purposes of explosions. Hence, if PNE's were not covered by a test ban treaty, Nuclear-Weapon States could use them to test their nuclear stockpile, and to improve the functioning of new warheads. Non-nuclear weapons States could develop basic nuclear explosives capabilities and therefore the ability to produce nuclear weapons. The paper concluded that the "uncontrolled use and development of nuclear explosions for peaceful purposes is incompatible with the objectives of a comprehensive test ban." [37]

Although UK declared its preference to ban all nuclear explosions, it acknowledged the possibility of a separate arrangement for peaceful nuclear explosions, as long as it prohibited PNE's at the time that the comprehensive test ban entered into force.[38] This view was shared by Sweden and Japan. They called for either a prohibition of all nuclear explosions, or an agreement on an international supervision and control system.[39] Some of the observers of the Conference also shared this view.[40]

In a less compromising position Australia stated that "the most effective and safest solution is to ban all nuclear tests"[41] and proposed a scope for a treaty which reads:

> "Each Party to this Treaty undertakes not to carry out any nuclear weapons test explosion or any other nuclear explosion.

"Each Party to this Treaty undertakes, furthermore, to refrain from causing, encouraging, assisting, permitting or in any other way participating in the carrying out of any nuclear weapons test explosion or any other nuclear explosion.

"Each Party to this Treaty undertakes to take all necessary measures to prohibit and prevent any activity in violation of the provisions of the Treaty anywhere under its jurisdiction or control."[42]

(b) A Second view that emerged in the discussion of PNE's was that a comprehensive test ban treaty should cover only nuclear weapons test explosions but a protocol should accompany the treaty establishing a moratorium on PNE's until a suitable arrangement could be found. This view was advocated mainly by States of the Socialist group and was reflected in various proposals [43] for a subsidiary body, as well as in two drafts treaties.

The first draft treaty was submitted by USSR in 1983.[44] Its scope required:

"Each State party to this Treaty shall undertake to prohibit, to prevent, and not to carry out any nuclear weapon test explosion at any place under its jurisdiction and control, in any environment - in the atomsphere, beyond its limits, including outer space, under water or under ground.

"A moratorium shall be declared on nuclear explosions for peaceful purposes, under which the parties to this Treaty shall refrain from causing, encouraging, or in any other way participating in carrying out such explosions until the relevant procedure has been evolved."

The second draft treaty was submitted in 1987 by a group of Socialist States including the Soviet Union.[45] The envisaged scope differed from the previous Soviet draft in the broader formulation of the paragraph concerning PNE's: "Provisons should be made for the formulation of a provision preventing the ban on nuclear weapon test explosions from being circumvented by means of peaceful nuclear explosions."

UK hinted at the fact that although an agreement for PNE's had been envisaged, there were no verification proposals which would offer the prospect of agreement being reached on measures permitting the continuation of PNE's under a CTBT.[46]

(c) A third view considered that a comprehensive test ban treaty should only cover nuclear weapons test explosions. This view was held mainly by certain members of the Group of 21. It was never clarified whether any form of control should be applied to PNE's. In 1990, Argentina and Brazil altered their positions in favour of a ban on all nuclear explosions.[47] This left India[48] as the only member of the CD favouring the exclusion of PNE's from the scope of a CTBT.

The arguments for separating PNE's from nuclear weapons tests were based on: the reference under the PTBT to discontinue "all test explosions of nuclear weapons for all time"; Article V of the NPT which states that any "potential benefits from any peaceful applications of nuclear explosions will be made available to non-nuclear weapons States"; the TTBT and PNET which distinguished between nuclear weapons and peaceful test explosions; and, the Tripartite Report of 1980 which agreed on a protocol establishing a moratorium on PNE's until other arrangements had been made.

Entry into Force of a Nuclear Test Ban Treaty

Since 1976, USSR had been insisting that a nuclear test ban treaty could enter into force only if all declared nuclear weapons powers participated. Since France and China had not been parties to any of the existing test limitation treaties, a number of countries felt that for an efficient nuclear test ban treaty, all nuclear weapons powers must cease testing. Four approaches were proposed to include all Nuclear-Weapon States in a comprehensive test ban treaty.

(a) The first approach was advocated by the Soviet Union which, after the failure of the tripartite negotiations in 1982, returned in part to its previous position and demanded all Nuclear-Weapon States to participate in a test ban agreement.[49]

(b) The second approach represented a modification of this position and was reflected in a draft treaty that USSR submitted in 1983.[50] The draft envisaged a treaty that would enter into force after its ratification by twenty governments, "including the Governments of all States permanent members of the Security Council"[51], which are the five declared nuclear weapons powers. However, the treaty might enter into force for a limited period, once UK, USA, and USSR had ratified the treaty.

(c) The third approach represented the latest position of the Soviet Union which, together with a group of Socialist States, presented a draft treaty in 1987.[52] The draft conceived the entry into force of the treaty following the ratification by an unspecified number of States (to be negotiated) but including USA and USSR. Five years after the entry into force of the treaty, a review conference would be convened that would decide whether the treaty was to remain in force and whether other nuclear weapons States would have to accede to the treaty if they had not done so.

(d) Sweden tabled a draft treaty in 1983[53] which envisaged a treaty that would enter into force after the ratification by twenty governments, including the Governments of UK, USA and USSR. However, the most recent statement of the Swedish delegation noted that an effective nuclear test ban required universal adherence.[54] Similar statements were made by a number of other States.[55]

Monitoring a Nuclear Test Ban Treaty

Among the members of the CD, it has been generally recognized that the basic elements of a monitoring system for a nuclear test ban treaty include: national technical means, an international exchange of seismic data, and procedures for on-site inspections.[56] The group of Scientific Experts, an ad hoc working group of the CD, proposed and elaborated an international seismic monitoring system which was considered the most important component of test-ban monitoring. In addition, various proposals were made for improvements of this system. The proposed seismic monitoring system was outlined in principle in three draft treaties submitted to the CD by USSR(1983), Sweden(1983) and a group of Socialist States (1987).[57] In addition to seismological techniques, the monitoring of ariborne radioactivity and on-site inspections were also considered.

The Group of Scientific Experts

The idea of a system of international co-operation for detecting underground nuclear explosions through an exchange of seismic data, dates back to a Swedish proposal of 1965.[58] This resulted in informal consultations which became known as the "detection club". These discussions, however, only provided information of national views on a seismic monitoring systems. In 1976, as a result of a Swedish initiative, the Conference of Committee on Disarmament(CCD) held several informal meetings on verification focussing particularly on a global seismic monitoring system. In recognizing the vital importance of technical expertise in addressing the issue of verification Sweden proposed the establishment of an ad hoc committee of government-appointed experts.[59] This proposal was adopted by the CCD towards the end of the session and was entitled "The Scientific Group of Experts to Consider International Cooperative Measures to Detect and Identify Seismic Events".

This group of scientists and representatives from several countries was mandated to elaborate procedures for the establishment and maintenance of an international seismological monitoring network for the verification of a comprehensive nuclear test ban. The Group proposed an international seismic monitoring network and experimented with the possibility of transmitting data on a global scale in 1984.

The Institutional Framework of the Ad Hoc Group

The Group of Scientific Experts was established in 1976 for the purpose of developing a concept of an international seismic monitoring system. This concept was presented in the Group's first report in 1978.[60] Subsequently, the CCD decided to continue the work of the ad hoc Group.[61] Its terms of reference were redefined on the assumption that a test ban treaty would prohibit all nuclear explosions:

> "The Ad-Hoc Group should continue its work by studying the scientific and methodological principals of a possible experimental test of a global network of seismological stations of the kind which might be established in the future for the international exchange of seismological data under a treaty prohibiting nuclear weapon tests, and a protocol covering nuclear

explosions for peaceful purposes which would be an integral part of the treaty."

In 1979, the CD decided on a mandate which has remained force until present.[62] The relevant part of the mandate reads :

"This work should, *inter alia*, include:
— further elaboration, with the second report of the Group as a basis, of detailed instructions for an experimental test of the global system for international cooperative measures to detect and identify seismic events;
— further development of the scientific and technical aspects of the global system;
— cooperation in the review and analysis of national investigations into relevant matters such as: the conditions for using the WMO Global Telecommunication Systems for seismic data exchange; procedures to obtain desired data at individual stations under a range of conditions; the analysis and data handling procedures at the envisaged data centres; and methods of rapid exchange of wave form data."

The work of the Group is carried out on an informal basis. After each of the sessions a formal progress report is submitted to the CD. The Group is open to scientific experts nominated by any CD member State, or upon invitation by the CD to any UN member State. It was agreed also to invite a representative of the World Meteorological Organization (WMO)[63]. Along with the extension of the members of the CD in 1979, the number of States participating in the ad hoc Group also increased.[64] The Group, however, has consisted mainly of countries with strong national seismological verification programme, and thus Africa and South America have been under-represented.[65]

In 1982, the ad hoc Group agreed to establish five study groups. In 1987, the study groups were adapted to meet the requirements of an updated version of the proposed seismic monitoring system.[66] The study groups are:

Study Group 1: Seismograph stations and Station networks.

Study Group 2: National Data Centres (NDC's)

Study Group 3: Data Exchange between National Data Centres (NDC's) and International Data Centres (IDC's) using the Global Telecommunication System of the World Meterological Organization (WMO/GTS)

Study Group 4: Data exchange between National Data Centres (NDC's) and International Data Centres (IDC's) using communications channels other than WMO/GTS

Study Group 5: International Data Centres (IDC's)

Several proposals have been made to expand the mandate of the Scientific Group of Experts. A broader mandate might include technical questions of a global system for monitoring airborne radioactivity, satellite imagery or on-site inspections. Presently, there has been no consensus in the Scientific Group of Experts for the consideration of verification techniques other than seismological.

Notes and References

1. General Assembly resolution S-102, paras.45-51.
2. CD/756. The document is reproduced in *The UN Yearbook*, Vol.12: 1987, chapter VIII, annex. The earlier initiative, in 1982, was contained in document A/37/243 and led to

resolution 37/85, to which the text was annexed, See *The UN Yearbook*, Vol.7:1982, chapter X.
3. A/41/518-S/18277, attachment. The document is reproduced in *The UN Yearbook*, Vol.II:1986, chapter VIII, annex.
4. A/43/58. annex. sec. I.
5. A/44/211.
6. Article II of the Treaty Banning Nuclear Weapon Tests in the Atmosphere, in Outer Space and under Water (PTBT) reads:

Article II

1. Any Party may propose amendments to this Treaty. The text of any proposed amendment shall be submitted to the Depositary Governments, which shall circulate it to all Parties to this Treaty. Thereafter, if requested to do so by the one-third or more of the Parties, the depositary Governments shall convene a conference, to which they shall invite all the Parties, to consider such amendments.

2. Any amendment to this Treaty must be approved by a majority of the votes of all the Parties to this Treaty, including the votes of all of the Original Parties. The amendments shall enter into force for all Parties upon the deposit of instruments of ratification by a majority of all the Parties, including the instruments of ratification of all of the Original parties.

The full text of the Treaty appears in *Status of Multilateral Arms Regulation and Disarmament Agreements*, 3rd edition: 1987 (United Nations publication, Sales No. E.88IX.5).

6a. The discussion is based on the UNDIR study by Thomas Schmalberger: 'In pursuit of Nuclear Test Ban Treaty: A Guide to Debate in the Conference on Disarmament', United Nations Institute for Disarmament Research, UN, New York, 1991, pp.49-63.

7. See 'Rules of Procedures of the Committee on Disarmament', in Official Records of the General Assembly, Thirty-fourth Session, Supplement No.27, (A/34/27), Vol.I, Appendix I.

8. When no progress in the search for consensus on a mandate was achieved, several attempts were undertaken to change the rule of consensus in such a way as to enable the establishment of subsidiary organs for the effective performance of the functions of the CD. None of these attempts were successful. See, e.g., CD/204, (Mexico, Nigeria, Pakistan,

Sweden and Yugoslavia), 'Establishment of Subsidiary Organs', CD/PV.134 (Mexico), CD/PV.192, (Group of 21), 'Statement by the Group of 21 (Item 1: Nuclear Test Ban)'.

9. See, e.g.,CD/PV.275 (German Democratic Republic), CD/PV.276 (Algeria), CD/PV.301 (USSR), CD/PV.351 (German Democratic Republic).

10. CD/492 (Group of 21), 'Draft Mandate for the (Ad Hoc Subsidiary Body) on a Nuclear Test Ban', in its updated version CD/520, CD/520/Rev. 1, CD/520/Rev.2, (Group of 21), 'Draft Mandate for the Ad-Hoc Committee on a Nuclear Test Ban'.

11. CD/434 Memorandum of a Group of Socialist States, 'Organizational Matters of the Work of the Conference on Disarmament', p.2; in its updated version CD/522, CD/522/Rev.1, (Group of Socialist States), 'Draft Mandate for an Ad Hoc Committee on Item 1 of the Agenda of the Conference on Disarmament Submitted by a Group of Socialist States'.

12. CD/259 (German Democratic Republic), 'Draft Mandates for Ad-Hoc Working Groups on a Nuclear Test Ban, and the cessation of the Nuclear Arms Race and Nuclear Disamament' was submitted in 1982 and was endorsed by Bulgaria, Czechoslovakia and Mongolia (CD/PV.166 (Bulgaria), CD/PV.167 (Czechoslovakia) and CD/PV.166 (Mongolia).

13. CD/438, (Mexico), 'Draft Mandate For The Ad Hoc Subsidiary Body On A Nuclear Test Ban'.

14. CD/629 (Bulgaria, German Democratic Republic), 'Working Paper on Item One of the Agenda of the Conference on Disarmament Entitled Nuclear Test Ban.'

15. CD/PV.375 (Mexico); the proposal was based on the General Assembly resolution A/RES/40/80A.

16. CD/772 (Indonesia, Kenya, Mexico, Peru, Sri Lanka, Sweden, Venezuela and Yugoslavia), 'Draft Mandate for an Ad Hoc Committee on Item One of the Agenda of the Conference on Disarmament.'

17. CD/829 (Group of 21), 'Draft Mandate for an Ad Hoc Committee on Item One of the Agenda of the Conference on Disarmament.'

18. In 1987, the United States and the Soviet Union started bilateral negotiations on verification provisions for the TTBT and the PNET which were decisive for the entry into force of the two treaties. The negotiations were part of the bilateral meetings of US-USSR nuclear testing experts, which had

started in 1986. Although no formal mandate proposal was submitted, USSR stated that bilateral efforts alone could not provide a final solution to the problem of nuclear tests and stressed that the preparation of a CTBT should be undertaken concurrently in the CD—(CD/PV.430(USSR). To that end the Soviet Union together with a Group of Socialist States submitted a draft treaty to the CD. A similar position was taken by a number of non-aligned States which felt that bilateral talks would not offer an acceptable substitute to negotiations in the Conference. See, e.g., CD/PV.406 (Pakistan), CD/PV.432 (Sweden). USA on the other hand, appealed to the Conference to complement these negotiations by establishing a subsidiary body with a non-negotiating mandate instead of competing with these bilateral efforts — CD/PV.408 (United States), CD/PV.417 (United States.)

19. CD/181 (Group of 21), 'Statement by the Group of 21 on Item 1 of the Agenda of the Committee on Disarmament Entitled: Nuclear Test Ban'; this statement was based on previous proposal of the Group of 21, namely, CD/72 and CD/134.

20. CD/194 (Group of Socialist Countries), 'Statement of a Group of Socialist countries Concering a Nuclear Test Ban.'

21. See,e.g.,CD/PV.65 (Canada), CD/PV.66(Italy), CD/PV.81 (Netherlands), CD/PV.137(United States), CD/PV.209 (United States), CD/PV.209 (Australia), CD/PV.209 (Belgium), CD/PV.209 (United Kingdom), CD/PV.209 (Italy),

22. CD/521, (Australia, Belgium, Canada, Federal Republic of Germany, Italy, Japan, Netherlands, United Kingdom and United States of America), 'Draft Mandate for the Ad-Hoc Subsidiary Body on Item 1 of the Agenda of the Conference on Disarmament entitled "Nuclear Test Ban".'

23. CD/PV.194 (Pakistan).

24. CD/PV.308 (Sri Lanka), CD/PV.297 (Sweden).

25. CD/PV.279 (Australia), CD/PV.292 (Australia), CD/PV.294 (Australia).

26. CD/621 (Australia, Belgium, Federal Republic of Germany, Italy, Japan,Netherlands, Norway, United Kingdom, United States of America),'Draft Program of Work for an Ad Hoc Committee on Item One of the Agenda of the Conference on Disarmament Entitled "Nuclear Test Ban".'

27. CD/PV.164 (The Chairperson); the drafting group comprised

Brazil, Bulgaria, the German Democratic Republic, India, Japan, Nigeria, the United States of America and Yugoslavia.

28. In 1983, the CD decided to re-establish all ad hoc committees of the previous year based on their former mandates. For the ad hoc committee on a nuclear test ban, it was agreed to consider the possible revision of the mandate but this did not lead to consensus. The ad hoc committee of 1983 therefore continued to work with its previous mandate of 1982. (CD/358, 'Decision on the re-establishment of ad-hoc working groups for the 1983 session of the Committee on Disarmament'. See also CD/PV.209 (Chairperson), CD/PV.212 (Chairperson).

29. CD/291, 'Decision adopted by the Committee on Disarmament on the establishment of an ad-hoc working group under item 1 of its agenda entitled "Nuclear Test Ban".'

30. CD/PV.178 (Burma), CD/PV.179 (German Democratic Republic), CD/PV.277 (Pakistan), CD/PV.180 (Romania), CD/PV.182 (Sweden), CD/PV.181 (USSR), CD/PV.180 (Venezuela).

31. See,e.g.,CD/PV.178 (Sweden).

32. See,e.g.,CD/PV.187 (Bulgaria), CD/PV.237 (Australia), CD/PV.237 (Pakistan).

33. CD/PV.178 (Sweden), CD/PV.187 (Sweden), CD/PV.236 (German Democratic Republic).

34. CD/332 'Report of the Ad-Hoc Working Group on a 'Nuclear Test Ban'.

35. CD/312 (CD/NTB/WP.1) (Netherlands), 'Nuclear Test Ban'.

36. Another argument was raised that all possible methods and qualitative improvements for testing, such as laboratory tests and simulation techniques, should also be considered. Although some delegations acknowledged the advancements in laboratory technology, they rejected this view referring to a UN Study which stated that a CTB could not cover laboratory tests because they were beyond verification capabilities—CD/86, 'Letter dated 24 March 1980 from the Secretary General of the United Nations to the Chairman of the Committee on Disarmament transmitting the Report on a Comprehensive Nuclear Test Ban, prepared pursuant to General Assembly Decision 32/44 of 11 December 1979'.

37. CD/383 (CD/NTB/WP.3) (United Kingdom), 'Peaceful Nuclear Explosions in Relation to a Nuclear Test Ban', p.3.

38. ibid, p.2; see also CD/PV.186 (United Kingdom), CD/PV.219

(United Kingdom), CD/PV.230 (United Kingdom), CD/PV.237 (United Kingdom).

39. CD/388 (Japan), 'Verificatin and Compliance of a Nuclear Test Ban'. The Swedish draft treaty was submitted in 1983 as CD document CD/381 (Sweden), 'Draft Treaty Banning any Nuclear Weapon Test Explosion in Any Environment') and was based on a previous draft treaty which Sweden had tabled to the CCD in 1977 as CCD document CCD/526 and Rev. 1(CCD/526 and Rev.1, 'Draft Treaty Banning Nuclear Weapon Test Explosions in all Environments'.

40. See, e.g., CD/PV.244 (Norway), CD/PV.296 (New Zealand, (CD/PV.298 (Finland), CD/PV.342 (Finland), CD/PV.343 (Norway).

41. CD/PV.241 (Australia).

42. CD/405 (CD/NTB/WP.8) (Australia), 'Proposal for the Scope of a Comprehensive Nuclear Test Ban Treaty'; see also CD/531 (Australia), 'Principles for the Verification of a Comprehensive Nuclear Test Ban Treaty'.

43. See, e.g., CD/629 (People's Republic of Bulgaria, German Democratic Republic), 'Working Paper on Item One of the Agenda of the Conference on Disarmament Entitled "Nuclear Test Ban'; CD/701 (Socialist Countires), 'Negotiations on a Treaty on the Complete and General Prohibition of Nuclear Weapon Tests', CD/743 (Bulgaria, Czechoslovakia, German Democratic Republic, Hungary, Mongolia, Poland, Romania, Union of Soviet Socialist Republics), 'Nuclear Test Ban'; CD/746 (German Democratic Republic), 'Nuclear Test Ban".

44. CD/346, "Letter dated 14 February 1983 from the Representative of the Union of Soviet Socialist Republics to the Committee on Disarmament transmitting the 'Basic Provisions of a Treaty on the Complete and General Prohibition of Nuclear Weapon Tests'."

45. CD/756, "Letter dated 8 June 1987 from the Representatives of Bulgaria, Czechoslovakia, the German Democratic Republic, Hungary, Mongolia, Poland, Romania and the Union of Soviet Socialist Republics, Addressed to the President of the Conference on Disarmament transmitting the Text of the 'Basic Provisions of a Treaty on the Complete and General Prohibition of Nuclear Weapon Tests'."

46. CD/383 (CD/NTB/WP.3) (United Kingdom), 'Peaceful Nuclear Explosions in Relation to a Nuclear Test Ban'; see also CD/

402, (CD/NTB/WP.7) (United Kingtom), 'Verification Aspects of a Comprehensive Test Ban Treaty (CTBT)'.
47. CD/PV.574 (Argentina and Brazil).
48. CD/PV.575 (India).
49. See, e.g., CD/PV.181 (USSR), CD/PV.222(USSR).
50. CD/346, "Letter dated 14 February 1983 from the Representative of the Union of Soviet Socialist Republics to the Committee on Disarmament transmitting the 'Basic Provisions of a Treaty on the Complete and General Prohibition of Nuclear Weapon Tests'."
51. ibid, 33.
52. CD/756, "Letter dated 8 June 1987 from the Representatives of Bulgaria, Czechoslovakia, the German Democratic Republic, Hungary, Mongolia, Poland, Romania and the Union of Soviet Socialist Republics, Addressed to the President of the Conference on Disarmament transmitting the Text of the 'Basic Provisions of a Treaty on the Complete and General Prohibition of Nuclear Weapon Tests'."
53. CD/381, 'Draft Treaty Banning any Nuclear Weapon Test Explosin in any Environment'.
54. CD/PV.555 (Sweden).
55. CD/PV.574 (Argentina and Brazil), CD/PV.497 (Australia), CD/PV.537 (Hungary), CD/PV.575 (India,), CD/PV.506 (Pakistan), CD/PV.487 (Romania).
56. CD/412, p.6; see also CD/384 (CD/NTB/WP.4) (Australia, 'Institutional Arrangements for a CTB Verification System; An Illustrative List of Questions'), and CD/388 (Japan), 'Verificatin and Compliance of a Nucleaar Test Ban'.
57. CD/346 "Letter dated 14 February 1983 from the Representative of the Union of Soviet Socialist Republics to the Committee on Disarmament transmitting the 'Basic Provisions of a Treaty on the Complete and General Prohibition of Nuclear Weapon Tests'", CD/381, 'Draft Treaty Banning any Nuclear Weapon Test Explosion in any Environment'; CD/756, "Letter dated 8 June 1987 from the Representatives of Bulgaria, Czechoslovakia, the German Democratic Republic, Hungary, Mongolia, Poland, Romania and the Union of Soviet Socialist Republics, addressed to the President of the Conference on Disarmament transmitting the Text of the 'Basic Provisions of a Treaty on the Complete and General Prohibition of Nuclear Weapon Tests'."

58. ENDC/154 (Sweden), 'Memorandum on International Cooperation for the Detection of Underground Nuclear Explosions'.

59. CCD/482 (Sweden), 'Working Paper on Cooperative International Measures to Monitor a CTB'; CCD/495 (Sweden), 'Terms of Reference for a Group of Scientific Governmental Experts to Consider International Cooperative Measures to Detect and Identify Seismic Events'; see also CCD/PV.704 (Sweden).

60. CCD/558, 'Letter dated 9 March 1978 from the Chairman of the Ad Hoc Group of Scientific Experts to Consider International Cooperative Measures to Detect and to Identify Seismic Events to the Co-Chairman of the Conference of the Committee on Disarmament Transmitting the Final Report of the Ad-Hoc Group'.

61. The CCD followed the advice of the Ad Hoc Group stated in their final report, a Japanese suggestion (CCD/PV.733 Japan) and a Swedish proposal (CD/562 (Sweden). 'Terms of Reference for the Continued Work of the CCD Ad-Hoc Group of Scientific Experts to Consider International Cooperative Measures to Detect and to Identify Seismic Events').

62. CD/PV.48.

63. CD/PV.11; at the Eighth Congress of the WMO in 1979 it was agreed, in principle, that the WMO should assist the United Nations in the use of the Global Telecommunication System (GTS), and to direct its Executive Committee to study the matter.

64. Australia, Bulgaria, Canada, Czechoslovakia, German Democratic Republic, Federal Republic of Germany, Egypt, Hungary, India, Italy, Japan, Mexico, Netherlands, Poland, Sweden, Union of Soviet Socialist Republics, United Kingdom and United States of America sent scientists or representatives to the Ad-Hoc Group. In subsequent sessions Argentina, Belgium, China, India, Iran Kenya, Pakistan and Romania joined the Ad-Hoc Group temporrily or permanently. Upon their request Austria, Denmark, Finland, New Zealand and Norway, Switzerland and Turkey participated as observers in the Ad-Hoc Group temporarily or permanently.

65. Only India, Egypt and Peru sent experts.

66. CD/318, 'Progress Report to the Committee on Disarmament on the Fourteenth Session of the Ad-Hoc Group of Scientific Experts to Consider International Cooperative Measures to

Detect and Identify Seismic Events'; CD/778, 'Progress Report to the Committee on Disarmament on the Fourteenth Session of the Ad-Hoc Group of Scientific Experts to Consider International Cooperative Measures to Detect and Identify Seismic Events'.

Chapter 4
Prelude to Current Phase of Negotiations

Partial Test Ban Treaty Amendment Conference

In 1990 agreement was reached to convene an Amendment Conference of the State Parties to the Treaty from 7 to 18 January 1991. The Conference is discussed in the following section.

The UN General Asembly resolutions on the Amendment Conference not only drew negative votes from the United Kingdom and the United States, but also 28 abstentions, indicating important reservations about this recent approach towards achievement of a test ban. The two traditional resolutions, sponsored, respectively, by mainly non-aligned countries led by Mexico, and by Australia and New Zealand also received negative votes by the three Western nuclear Powers in the case of the former, and in the case of the latter, by two of them — France and the United States — with the United Kingdom abstaining. In all, it appeared at the beginning of 1991 that there remained serious obstacles to be overcome before complete cessation of nuclear explosions could be achieved.

At the request of more than one-third of the parties to the Partial Test Ban Treaty, the Amendment Conference[1] was convened in New York from 8 to 17 January 1991 by the depositary Governments in accordance with the provisions of article II and pursuant to General Assembly resolutions and to decisions of the parties.[2] One hundred of the 117 State Parties participated.[3] Following the opening of the Conference by the President of the 1990 Meeting of the State Parties for the Organization of the Amendment Conference, Ambassador Jayasinghe of Sri Lanka, the Secretary-General of the United Nations delivered an opening statement.

In his remarks, the Secretary-General emphasized the ongoing rapid transformation of the global political landscape and recent, positive achievements in the disarmament and security fields as well as continuing crisis. Affirming his support of a comprehensive test ban, he urged the participants to work towards that end. He felt that the Conference provided an opportunity for a constructive endeavour to advance prospects for such a ban. He also commented on the importance of a revitalized multilateral disarmament process.

At the opening meeting, Ali Altas, Minister for Foreign Affairs of Indonesia, was acclaimed President of the Conference. Ali Altas observed that realization of the goal set 27 years earlier—the banning of all tests — was more than overdue. He felt that the major questions of verification of a test ban and confidence in the reliability and safety of existing weapons had been resolved by technological means, and what was needed was political determination to move ahead. After decades of failure, the amendment procedure contained in the Partial Test Ban Treaty had appeared as the remaining avenue open in a world in which multilateral co-operation had become a necessity.

President Gorbachev of the Soviet Union conveyed a message to the Conference reiterating his country's support of a comprehensive test ban without delay as well as its readiness to stop nuclear tests at any time if the United States did likewise, and to agree to the amendment of the Partial Test Ban Treaty.

In the General debate, a large majority of the 63 representatives who addressed the Conference supported the proposal to amend the Partial Test Ban Treaty to make it into an adequately verifiable, comprehensive test-ban instrument. Mexico, the initiator and chief sponsor of the approach, made observations about the continual underground testing by the three depositary States of the Partial Test Ban Treaty and about the apparent resolution, by the two major depositary Powers, of the questions of verification and compliance in the context of their Threshold Test Ban Treaty and Peaceful Nuclear Explosions Treaty. Mexico felt that clarification of the depositaries' positions was one of the tasks of the Conference. Other tasks were to facilitate accession to the future treaty and to consider sanctions to be applied in cases of its violations. Mexico, among numerous others, held that the Conference provided a unique multilateral forum for the international community to achieve a complete cessation of nuclear testing.

Other speakers recognized various difficulties in achieving the objective of a complete halt to testing through the Conference. Several participants, including sponsors of the amendment approach, saw it at the least as requiring two or more sessions of the Conference. Others regarded the Conference as a milestone on the way to a complete test ban. Still others felt that the importance of the Conference lay in its potential to focus attention, mould public opinion and provide an impetus to endeavours to achieve that goal. A number of participants, including those Western and associated States that regarded the approach as impractical, saw the Conference as providing a worthwhile opportunity for the airing and clarification of views. Those holding that opinion identified the Conference on Disarmament, in which all the Nuclear-Weapon States were represented, as the appropriate forum for the negotiation of a verifiable comprehensive test ban treaty.

The Soviet Union, for its part, felt that achievement of a nuclear test-ban was a priority issue, and that therefore all possible efforts, both bilateral and multilateral, should be pursued in parallel. It attached importance to both the Soviet-American step-by-step process and the work of the Conference on Disarmament, as well as to the Amendment Conference itself. It was among those which felt that the Conference brought global attention to the need for a complete cessation of tests and could provide an impetus for specific ideas. Other speakers, however, including those of the United States and the United Kingdom, which had voted consistently against the approach of holding a Conference to amend the Treaty, while reiterating their commitment to a comprehensive test ban, stressed that the matter could not be considered in isolation from the continuing need for reliance on a nuclear deterrent. Both these countries and many others made clear their support of further work on the complex issues relating to a nuclear-test ban in the Conference on Disarmament. The United States in particular questioned whether the amendment approach was in the best interests of the existing Partial Test Ban Treaty and its parties; it believed it was not. It made clear that it would not participate in or provide financial support to any continuation of the Conference.

In view of the divergent positions on the practicality of amending the Partial Test Ban Treaty and of negotiating a ban in the Conference on Disarmament, it was not possible to reach consensus on the agenda item, 'Consideration of the proposed amendment to the Treaty Banning Nuclear Weapon Tests in the Atmosphere, in Outer Space and under Water as provided for in its article II, including reports of the Committees'.

When it became clear also that no consensus would be possible with regard to any extension, reconvening or resumption of the Amendment Conference, a draft decision sponsored by Indonesia, Mexico, Nigeria, Peru, the Philippines, Sri Lanka, the United Republic of Tanzania, Venezuela and Yugoslavia and, subsequently, Senegal was put to a vote. The draft decision, with an oral revision by the sponsors read out by the representative of Mexico, was adopted by a recorded vote of 74 to 2 (United Kingdom and United States), with 19 abstentions (Austria, Belgium, Bulgaria, Canada, Czechoslovakia, Finland, Germany, Greece, Hungary, Israel, Italy, Japan, Luxembourg, Netherlands, Poland, Romania, Spain, Switzerland, Turkey). It read as follows:

"Acknowledging the complex and complicated nature of certain aspects of a comprehensive test-ban treaty, especially those with regard to verification of compliance and possible sanctions against non-compliance, the State Parties were of the view that further work needed to be undertaken. Accordingly, they agreed to mandate the President of the Conference to conduct consultations with a view to achieving progress on those issues and resuming the work of the Conference at an appropriate time."

Fifteen participants spoke in explanation of their vote; three which voted in favour (Argentina, Philippines and Sweden), the two which voted negatively, and ten from among those which abstained. Most speakers regretted that a consensus outcome had not been possible, but felt that the Conference had provided an opportunity for a constructive airing of views. Several participants held firmly that the Conference on Disarmament, as the multilateral negotiating body, provided the proper forum through which to continue work towards a comprehensive test-ban. The United Kingdom and the United States maintained their stated positions, with the latter expressing its belief that the Amendment Conference had not contributed to the continued viability of the Partial Test Ban Treaty. The United States looked forward to a world in which nuclear arsenals could be reduced and the current degree of nuclear testing would not be required; and it would, therefore, contribute to efforts in the Conference on Disarmament related to a comprehensive test ban.

Regarding linkage between the CTBT and the NPT (Nuclear Non-Proliferation Treaty), three basic groups of positions could be identified among the states at the conference. The overlap between them notwithstanding, one group of states stressed the importance of a comprehensive test-ban for the future of the NPT but did not make the fate of the NPT hostage to a test ban. Sweden, Hungary, Austria, Belgium, Bulgaria, Cyprus, Romania and Switzerland belonged to this group. The second group pointed to the link between ending nuclear tests and the non-proliferation of nuclear weapons but also went further by stating that a total nuclear test-ban was an indispensable prerequisite for the survival of the NPT. Reflecting this concern were Egypt, Botswana, Cameroon, Mauritius, Mongolia, Syria and Zambia. A third group of states, however, rejected the notion of establishing too strong a link between the NPT and the CTBT which, according to them, stood firmly on its own merits and should not be linked to the resolution of other issues, however important they might be.

More interestingly, any linkage between CTBT issue and the NPT was strongly rejected by two of the three Depository states, namely, USA and UK. USA expressed the firm belief that further legal constraints on nuclear testing were not likely to affect motivations of the states seeking to acquire nuclear weapons or to inhibit their ability to do so. UK saw no reason why adherence to a CTBT in addition to the NPT would afford world security if it was not provided by adherence to the NPT. Both USA and UK expressed profound reservations about the whole amendment approach for both substantive and procedural reasons. USA made it clear that it did not support negotiations on a CTBT at this time. The Soviet Union, for its part, reiterated its readiness to stop nuclear tests at any time if USA did likewise and declared that it was ready to amend the PTBT so as to convert it into a CTBT. In its statement, the Soviet delegation called for a constructive "dualism" of bilateral and multilateral efforts to bring this about.

This position of the Depository states, of course, came in for strong criticism from a number of countries, namely, Nigeria, Mexico, India, Afghanistan, Brazil, Cyprus, Libya, Myanmar, Nepal, Sri Lanka, Syria, Togo, Venezuela, Yugoslavia and Zambia. The conference concluded that further work needed to be undertaken.

Review Conference of the NPT

This was almost a replica of what happened in the four review conferences of the NPT. At the first review conference, Mexico proposed that nuclear parties would suspend all nuclear tests for ten years as soon as the number of NPT parties reached 100 and would extend the moratorium by three years each time five more states became parties. The moratorium would become permanent as soon as other nuclear states agreed to become parties. The proposal was rejected by the nuclear-weapon powers.

At the second review conference in 1975, the call for a moratorium on tests was rejected by the powers engaged in trilateral talks, who insisted that a verifiable treaty was preferable. But even the establishment of a CD working group to negotiate a multilateral test ban could not be agreed to, in spite of the argument put forward by the non-nuclear weapon states (NNW's) that trilateral and multilateral negotiations could supplement each other. All USA could accept, after strenuous negotiations, was the creation of a CD group without fixing a specific date for its establishment and without giving it the mandate to draft a treaty. Neither could an agreement be reached on initiation of multilateral negotiations in the CD for nuclear disarmament.

Similar differences persisted on the issue of a comprehensive test-ban in the third review conference in 1980. Compromise was struck by a 'formula' which took note of: (a) the call by all non-nuclear weapon states (NNW's) for resumption in 1985 of negotiations on a comprehensive test-ban (CTB); (b) the opinion shared by UK and USA that priority should be given to deep cuts in nuclear weapons, rather than to a CTB which, however, remained a long-term goal; and (c) USSR's readiness to conclude the CTBT and the Soviet moratorium.

At the fourth review conference also USA and UK insisted on considering the issue of the CTBT as a long-term goal, but Mexico (as well as Iran) insisted that the link between the CTBT and NPT must be explicit, a position resisted by USA. A compromise was reportedly put forward by the Chairman of the Committee dealing with the issue: It read:

"The conference further recognised that the discontinuance of nuclear testing would play a central role in the future of the NPT. The conference stressed the significant importance placed upon negotiations, multilateral and bilateral, during the next five years to conclude a CTBT, again again calls for early action towards that objective by the Conference on Disarmament. The conference urges that the ad hoc committee on a nuclear test ban be given an appropriate mandate to pursue the objective of negotiations to conclude a comprehensive nuclear test ban treaty."

USA and USSR, however, wanted to add a paragraph contained in the original draft in which the conference would also note "the jointly declared statement of the USA and USSR to proceed with the step-by-step negotiations on further intermediate limitation on nuclear testing, having the ultimate objective of complete cessation of nuclear testing as part of an effective disarmament process."

Eight states, namely, Mexico, Iran, Indonesia, Nigeria, Peru, Sri Lanka, Venezuela and Yugoslavia, agreed to accept the Chairman's proposal without any amendment; the three Depositories and Australia, Canada and Poland insisted on retaining the disputed paragraphs. The conference ended without a final declaration.

Interestingly, USSR reaffirmed its readiness to enter at once into negotiations on a CTBT. It pointed to its then moratorium on testing (which had begun in the autumn of 1989) and affirmed its willingness to suspend all testing pending negotiations on a CTBT.

Other Developments

The only nuclear explosion carried out in 1993 was that conducted by China. France, Russia and USA abided by their unilaterally announced test moratoria throughout the year.

United States and United Kingdom

In 1992 the Bush Administration continued to oppose a CTB and no formal negotiations were held.[4] Under international and congressional pressure, however, the Administration officially changed its testing policy. In July 1992 the Administration announced that, for the next five years, USA would conduct no more than six tests per year and no more than three tests per year above 35 kt and that all tests would be conducted for 'safety and reliability' purposes.[5] Many critics in the US Congress argued that these were only cosmetic changes and successfully pushed through sweeping legislation limiting US nuclear tests.

On 2 October 1992, President Bush signed into law the Fiscal Year (FY) 1993 Energy and Water Development Appropriations Act,[6] which contained a provision mandating a permanent ban on all US nuclear tests after 1996, unless another country conducted tests after that date. Bush called the provision limiting tests 'highly objectionable' but decided not to veto the Bill because it included $517 million for the Superconducting Super Collider, an $8 billion project located in Texas, a key State in Bush's re-election report. During and after the Presidential campaign, however, Clinton indicated that he would support the nuclear test-ban legislation.[7]

The abovementioned Act states that "no underground test of nuclear weapons may be conducted by the USA after 30 September 1996, unless a foreign state conducts a nuclear test after this date."[8] The legislation required the suspension of all US tests from 1 October 1992 until at least 1 July 1993. For tests to be conducted between the end of the nine-month moratorium and the cut-off date, the Administration must submit reports to Congress. The three reports—which would cover the last quarter of FY 1993 and all of FYs 1994, 1995 and 1996 — required a description of all proposed tests and a plan for installing modern safety features (insensitive high explosives, enhanced detonation safety systems or file-resistant fissile material `pits') in the warheads slated for testing. Only those warheads that have been re-designed to include a modern safety feature which they previously did not have, in accordance with the reports submitted by the Adminstration, may be tested.

In the period covered by these three reports, between the end of the moratorium and the 1996 cut-off date, a

PRELUDE TO CURRENT PHASE OF NEGOTIATIONS 87

total of no more than 15 tests could be conducted, with no more than five in any one report period. All of these tests must be conducted for safety purposes except for one 'reliability test' per report period, which must be approved by Congress.[9] The United Kingdom, which also conducts its tests at the US Nevada Test Site, was permitted to conduct one test per report period, but each test would count towards the report period and overall test limits.

The law also directed the Administration to submit to Congress a schedule for the resumption of test talks with Russia and a "plan for achieving a multilateral comprehensive ban on the testing of nuclear weapons by 30 September 1996."[10]

UK which had been conducting its nuclear tests jointly with USA in Nevada since 1962, did not support the new US law limiting nuclear tests. In fact, in August 1992, before the US Congress passed the law, the British ambassador to the United States, Sir Robin Renwick, wrote to the legislation's Senate sponsors that the total of three tests allowed to UK under the legislation would be "insufficient to assure the safety of U.K. warheads for the indefinite future". He also said that UK "cannot exclude the need to modernize" its warheads and that "neither a moratorium nor the complete phasing out of testing, as currently contemplated" would allow Britain to maintain an "effective deterrent.[11] In November 1992, Viscount Cranborne, the British Under-Secretary for Defence, stated that the new US testing law was "unfortunate and misguided", arguing that Britain would need to continue testing not for the "safety of the Trident system" but for the safety of "future systems". [12]

Despite the criticism of the new US position on testing, Tristan Garel-Jones, the press spokesman for Prime Minister John Major, said in October that UK had "always accepted the long term goal of a comprehensive test ban to be achieved on a step-by-step basis" and that UK was not considering any alternative underground nuclear test site to the US site in Nevada.[13]

After China conducted a test on 5 October 1993 at Lop Nor, the White House expressed its regrets and urged Beijing to refrain from further tests and join 'a global moratorium'. The White House statement said that Clinton's decision on whether to resume testing would be based on "fundamental US national security interests, taking into account: the contribution further tests would make to improving the safety and reliability of the US arsenal in preparation for a Comprehensive Test Ban (CTB); the extent to which China and others have responded to the US appeal for a global moratorium on testing; progress in the CTB negotiations; the implications of further US nuclear tests on our broader non-proliferation objectives."[14]

This White House statement, combined with press reports citing anonymous Administration officials, suggested that USA had backed away from a commitment to an automatic resumption of testing which was implicit in the policy of "no-first-test" announced on 3 July 1993 by President Bill Clinton stating that he had decided to extend the US moratorium on nuclear tests which had been introduced nine months earlier.[15] The extended moratorium would last at least through September 1994, as long as no other state conducted a nuclear test. President Clinton also called on the other nuclear-weapon states to do the same. If another state did conduct a test during the US moratorium, the Prsident would "direct the Department of Energy(DoE) to prepare to conduct additional tests while seeking approval to do so from Congress."[16] The DoE was expected to maintain a capability to resume testing. On 14 March 1994, Clinton extended the US moratorium through September 1995.[17]

The US Congress had decided in 1992 that the US testing programme should be terminated by 30 September 1996 "unless a foreign state conducts a nuclear test after this date" but after a limited number of safety tests had been conducted. Three of these tests were probably earmarked for UK. President Clinton stated in July 1993 that his Administration had now determined that the US nuclear weapons were safe and reliable.[18]

As UK has conducted its nuclear tests jointly with USA since 1962 at the Nevada Test Site, the US moratorium also prevents UK from carrying out tests. UK has over the years held the view that, since it needs to carry out limited testing to maintain the safety of its nuclear arsenal, it supports a nuclear comprehensive test ban treaty(CTBT) only as a long-term goal. However, in August 1993 the British delegate to the Conference on Disarmament (CD) stated that UK was now fully committed to negotiations on a comprehensive test ban.[19]

During the Clinton Administration's internal debate in the spring of 1993 on the question whether to resume testing after the moratorium mandated by the Hatfield Amendment expired, UK, which conducts its tests at the US Nevada Test Site, lobbied the State Department to oppose a moratorium extension. In fact, it was reported that the next test scheduled at the Nevada Test Site before President Bush signed the legislation containing the Hatfield Amendment on 2 October 1992 was for UK.[20] After US announcement of July 1993, however, Britain has publicly accepted the US decision, albeit grudgingly.[21]

The United Kingdom had completed its tests on a warhead for the Trident II SLBM, but was interested in developing a version of that warhead with new safety features as well as warhead for a new air-launched weapon for its Torando aircraft.[22] In October 1993, however, UK decided to cancel its nuclear tactical air-to-surface missile programme, primarily for budgetary reasons.

In December 1993, while releasing classified information on the US nuclear weapon programme of the preceding 50 years, the Department of Energy (DoE) of USA disclosed that USA had conducted 204 more nuclear weapon tests than had been reported officially.[23] All these tests were carried out underground, at the Nevada Test Site, after the signing of the 1963 Partial Test Ban Treaty (PTBT). According to DoE officials, all data on nuclear tests carried out at the Nevada Test Site have now been declassified. The reason given for not making prior announcements of all the tests was that USA wanted to inhibit Soviet monitoring of its testing activities.

The DoE reported that all these tests were weapon-related and conducted in shafts. One of them, carried out in 1964, was a joint US-UK test. The DoE did not give exact yields, "in order to protect nuclear weapon design capabilities."[24] Accidental on-site release of radioactivity from the explosions was reported. No information of off-site radiation was provided, since all such releases of radiation, it was claimed, were announced when the releases occurred. Additional information regarding the depth of burial and exact time of the tests was also made available.[25]

Of these previously unannounced tests, 111 were already known to both US and Soviet/Russian seismologists who have studied data an seismic records on tests for many years.[26] The clandestine, unannounced tests reported by these experts have over the years been entered in the *SIPRI* tables on nuclear explosions.

Together with the US Department of Defense, the DoE also released classified information on the yields of the tests conducted in the Pacific Ocean — all atmospheric, or in four cases carried out under water—prior to the US-Soviet test moratorium of 1958-61.

Russia

In 1992 Russia adhered to the commitment made by former Soviet President Mikhail Gorbachev in October 1991 not to conduct nuclear tests for one year, and on 19 October 1992 President Yeltsin announced that Russia would extend its moratorium at least till 1 July 1993.[27] In November 1992 Yeltsin reiterated his support for the negotiation of a CTB treaty [28] and announced that he would urge China to join the nuclear-test moratorium.[29]

Yeltsin, however, under pressure from Russian nuclear-weapon laboratories, had called, on 27 February 1992, for preparations to be made at the Russian test site at Novaya Zemlya for a resumption of testing at a rate of two to four tests per year if the moratorium expired.[30] CIS military commander Marshal Shaposhnikov said in September 1992 that "If our partners in the West don't stop these nuclear explosions, I think we would have to part with the moratorium and resume nuclear testing, may be in a less intensive manner."[31] Defence Minister Grachev reiterated this in October, noting that after 1 July 1993 "everything will . . . depend on the American side." Grachev added that the Russian Parliament was under pressure from Russia's nuclear laboratories not to ban all nuclear testing.[32]

The Soviet Union/Russia has not conducted a nuclear explosion since October 1990. President Boris Yeltsin extended earlier Soviet/Russian test moratoria, and on 21 October 1993, as a reaction to the Chinese test, the Russian Government made a statement that it did not plan to resume its nuclear testing programme but reserved the right to reconsider its decision "if the situation in this sphere continues to develop unfavourably."[33]

Although his Ministers of Atomic Energy and Defence have suggested in the past that they would like to resume testing at Novaya Zemlya,[34] President Yeltsin has consistently supported an extension of the moratorium and the negotiation of a CTB. In addition to its publicly stated objective of curbing nuclear proliferation, Russia has both environmental and economic reasons for not testing. The US Central Intelligence Agency (CIA) said in 1993 that "domestic and Scandinavian environmental organizations have publicized concerns about radioactive pollution in the Russian Arctic area" partially due to testing, and added that "Russia would be hard pressed to devote the resources necessary for a full-fledged nuclear testing program given its current economic crisis."[35] Nuclear testing at the Semipalatinsk site in Kazakhstan is not an option for Russia because the Kazakh President closed that site in August 1991.[36]

France

In April 1992, France announced a nuclear-test moratorium till the end of 1992 and said that it would decide whether to resume testing in 1993 depending on other countries' testing practices. This announcement marked a significant departure from past French policy. For the previous three years, France had conducted more tests per year than any country except USA. Moreover, until 1992 France had opposed or abstained from resolutions in the UN General Assembly to ban nuclear testing. Noting that the announcement came just a month after the Socialists had suffered a serious defeat in regional and local French elections and that two environmentalists parties —the Greens and the Generation Ecologic—had gained in the polls, some observers suggested that the moratorium was motivated primarily by domestic politics.[37] On the other hand, France took several other important initiatives in 1992, including accession to the NPT, suggesting that the moratorium reflected a real change in the French leadership's thinking.

In November 1992, the then Foreign Minister Roland Dumas called for five-power talks on nuclear testing, proposing that China, France, Russia, the United Kingdom and USA "engage next in a common reflection on the question of nuclear tests."[38] In January 1993, President Francois Mitterrand said that France would extend its moratorium for as long as USA and Russia refrained from testing.[39] According to one account, a one or two-year suspension of French tests would not delay the pace of French nuclear modernization programmes since prospective tests were planned to develop warheads for the M-5 SLBM missile, which is not scheduled to be deployed until the year 2005.[40]

In a speech at the signing ceremony of Chemical Weapons Convention in Paris in January 1993, President Francois Mitterand stated that France would maintain the test moratorium announced in April 1992, as long as other states refrained from testing. He repeated this statement in early July 1993, after President Clinton's announcement of the extended US moratorium. However, the French Prime Minister as well as the National Assembly (Parliament) is not in favour of a test ban, and the Atomic Energy and Defence Departments are pushing for a resumption of the French testing programme, arguing that an extended moratorium would delay the new M-45 submarine-launched ballistic missile (SLBM) warhead and development of the warhead for the M-5 SLBM and the ASLP (Air-Sol-Longue Portee) missile. In December 1993, a parliamentary group established by the Defence Committee of the National Assembly to study the implications of a permanent cessation of testing on the French nuclear force presented a report stating that, since the French simulation technique was not yet sufficiently developed to replace ordinary testing,

France could not guarantee the function of its nuclear force if its nuclear testing programme was cancelled. The group envisaged approximately 20 more French nuclear tests.[41]

China

China made no demonstration to indicate that it was seriously interested in negotiating a CTBT. In response to the French statement of November 1992, however, a Chinese Foreign Ministry spokesman stated that the Chinese Government was willing to discuss nuclear-test issues with all the members of the Conference on Disarmament (CD), "within the existing framework of the conference".[42] China conducted as many tests in 1992 (two) as it had in the three previous years combined. On 21 May 1992, China conducted the largest underground test in the history of its underground nuclear testing programme.[43]

In March 1992, when it acceded to the NPT, Chine appeared to lay down conditions for CTB participation, saying that states with the largest nuclear arsenals, such as the United States and Russia, should take the lead in "halting ... testing, production, deployment ... and drastically reducing those weapons." After "tangible progress" by those states, Beijing would be prepared to participate in a nuclear disarmament conference.[44]

According to intelligence reports, China had been preparing for a nuclear explosion for over a year when it conducted an explosion on 5 October 1993. Reconnaissance satellite pictures had shown that construction work for an underground nuclear explosion was going on at the Chinese test site in the Lop Nor area, in north-western China.[45] The 1993 Chinese test was the 39th nuclear explosion conducted by China since its nuclear testing programme started in 1964. The blast was detected by over 70 seismic stations throughout the world. According to the Swedish National Defence Research Establishment (FOA), the body wave magnitude was 6.4, which in this environment would be equivalent to a yield of approximately 80-160 kt.

The Chinese explosion evoked strong criticism from all over the world, especially from the other acknowledged nuclear-weapons states. However, none of them terminated its moratorium.

Notes and References

1. The report of the Amendment Conference was issued as document PTBT/CONF/13/Rev.1.
2. Resolutions 44/106 and 45/50 and various decisions taken by the parties to the Treaty in informal consultations and in their Meeting for the Organization of the Amendment Conference, held in New York from 29 May to 8 June 1990.
3. Afghanistan, Antigua and Barbuda, Argentina, Australia, Austria, Bahamas, Bangladesh, Belgium, Benin, Bhutan, Bolivia, Botswana, Brazil, Bulgaria, Byelorussian Soviet Socialist Republic, Canada, Cape Verde, Chile, Colombia, Costa Rica, Cote d'Ivoire, Cyprus, Czechoslovakia, Denmark, Dominican Republic, Ecuador, Egypt, El Salvador, Fiji, Finland, Gabon, Gambia, Germany, Greece, Guatemala, Hounduras, Hungary, Iceland, India, Indonesia, Iran (Islamic Republic of), Iraq, Ireland, Israel, Italy, Japan, Jordan , Kenya, Lao People's Democratic Republic, Lebanon, Libyan Arab Jamahiriya, Luxembourg, Malawi, Malaysia, Malta, Mauritius, Mexico, Mongolia, Morocco, Myanmar, Nepal, Netherlands, New Zealand, Nicargua, Nigeria, Norway, Pakistan, Papua New Guinea, Peru, Philippines, Poland, Republic of Korea, Romania, Samoa, Senegal, Seychelles, Spain, Sri Lanka, Sudan, Swaziland, Sweden, Switzerland, Syrian Arab Republic, Thailand, Togo, Trinidad and Tobago, Tunisia, Turkey, Uganda, Ukranian Soviet Socialist Republic, Union of Soviet Socialist Republics, United Kingdom of Great Britain and Northern Ireland, United Republic of Tanzania, United State of America, Uruguay, Venezuela, Yemen, Yugoslavia, Zaire and Zambia.

4. CTB talks held in Geneva among USA, UK and USSR were adjourned in Nov. 1980. The Reagan Administration formally withdrew from the CTB talks in 1982.
5. Gordon, M., 'US tightens limits on nuclear tests', *New York Times*, 15 July 1992, p.A1; see also Perth, J., 'Nuclear testing ban won't aid arms control', *Wireless File*, No.136 (15 July 1992), pp.2-3.
6. For the text of the Act, see 'US Congres nuclear testing limits', Institute for Defense and Disarmament Studies (IDDS), *Arms Control Reporter*, sheet 608.D.1-2, Oct.1992; Congressional Record, 24 Sep. 1992. p.H9424.
7. 'Remarks by Governor Bill Clinton, A roundtable discussion with employees of Sandia National Laboratories, Albaquacque, N.M. 18 September 1992'. Transcript from Clinton-Gore Campaign. P.9: Letter dated 12 Feb.1993, from President Bill Clinton to Senate Majority Leader George Mitchell, Congressional Record, 16 Feb.1993 p.S1513; Smith, R.J. 'Environmental Clean up role considered for A-weapons lab', *Washington Post*, 9 March, 1993, p.A10.
8. Due to a drafting error, the legislation also cited 1 Jan. 1997 as a cut-off date, but the language in the Act appears to prohibit testing after 30 Sept 1996.
9. While it was clearly the intent of the legislation's sponsors to have the reliability tests count towards the limit of 15 tests, some Bush Administration officials interpreted the legislation differently, that is, a total of 18 tests could be conducted, with 15 tests for safety and 3 more for reliability.
10. See n. 19 *infra*.
11. 'Text of letter sent from British Embassy Washington to Senators Hatfield, Mitchell, and Exon in August 1992'. British American Security Information Council (BASIC) Report No.28 (18 Feb 1993), p.5; *Arms Control Today*, Mar.1993. p.29.
12. British American Security Information Council (BASIC), 'A Comprehensive Test Ban Treaty: Britain's Public Position', Jan.1993, p.4; see also 22 Feb. 1993 letter from Congressman Mike Kopetski to Prime Minister John Major.
13. Written Answers, House of Commons, Parliamentary Debates, Official Report, 23 Oct.1992, cols. 407 and 408.
14. White House Statement, 5 October 1993; see also Lockwood. D., 'China's Nuclear test prompts US, others to review test policies', *Arms Control Today*, Nov.1993, p.20.

PRELUDE TO CURRENT PHASE OF NEGOTIATIONS

15. See, for example, Zamora-Collina, T. 'China bucks ban with bang', *Bulletin of the Atomic Scientists*, Dec.1993 p.3.
16. 'Moratorium extended on US nuclear testing', US Department of State Dispatch, Vol.4 No.28 (12 July 1993), p.501.
17. 'US extends moratorium on nucleaer testing', Wireless File (United States Information Services, US Embassy: Stockholm, 15 March 1994,) p.7.
18. US Department of State Dispatch (note 2).
19. Conference on Disarmament document CD/PV.658, 5 Aug.1993 pp.12-14.
20. *Trust and Verify*, Bulletin of the Verification Technology Information Centre (VERTIC), No.32 (Oct.1992), p.1.
21. For a compilation of quotations from the British Government on Nuclear testing, see British American Security Information Council (BASIC), 'UK response to US testing moratorium—cautious but supportive' (BASIC): London, 16 July 1993).
22. See, for example, Congressman John Spratt, Congressional Record, 29 Sept.1993, p.E2279.
23. Openness Press Conference. Fact Sheets (US Department of Energy: Washington DC, 7 Dec.1993).
24. Ibid.
25. Ibid.
26. The original research was carried out by Riley R. Geary, Seismological Laboratory of the California Institute of Technology.
27. *ITAR-TASS*, 'Yeltsin extends nuclear test moratorium', p.1, in FBIS-SOV 92-202, 19 Oct 1992, p.2; 'Text of decree extending nuclear test moratorium', *Rossiyskaya Gayata*, 21 Oct 1992. FBIS-SOV-92-205, 22 Oct.1992, p.12.
28. Robinson E. 'Yeltsin vows to remain in control', *Washington Post*, 11 Nov. 1992, p.A31.
29. Pollack, A. 'Yeltsin Plans end to A-sub Program', *New York Times*, 20 Nov. 1992, p.A10.
30. 'Secret decree may reopen nuclear test site'. *Nezavisimaya Gayata*, 24 March, 1992, p.6 in FBIS-SOV-92-060, 27 Mar1992, p.1; 'Preparations at nuclear test site 'going ahead'. *Rossiyskaya Gazeta*, 18 June 1992, p.2., in FBIS-SOV-92-121, 23 June 1992, p.4; Higgins, A., 'Yeltsin orders resumption of nuclear testing', *The Independent*, 15 April 1992.

31. Shargorodsky, S. "Russia missiles aimed at US, Marshal Says', *Boston Globe*, 26 September 1992.
32. Hiatt, F. 'Russia extends test ban', *Washington Post*, 14 Oct 1992, pp.1 and 25, see also Burbyga, N. 'Inspection in Novagaya Zemilya', *Izvestia*, 25 Sep. 1992, p.2 in FBIS-SOV-92-190, 30 Sep. 1992, p.3.
33. 'Government statement on China's nuclear test, Text of Statement', *FBIS-SOV-93-203*, 22 Oct.1993.
34. See, for example, Hiatt, F., 'Russia extends test ban', *Washington Post*, 14 Oct,1992, pp.1, 24; Burbyga, N. 'Inspection in Novaya Zemlya', *Izvestia*, 25 Sep. 1992, p.2., in FBIS-SOV 92-190, 30 Sep.1992 p.3; G-7 talks on nuclear moratorium may meet resistence', *Kommersant Daily*, 9 July 1993, p.4, in FBIS-SOV-93-131, 12 July 1993, p.16.
35. Proliferation Threats of the 1990s, Hearing before the Committee on Governmental Affairs, US Senate, 103rd Congress, Senate hearing 103-208 (US Government Printing Office: Washington, DC, 1993, p.147.
36. 'President's decree closing Semipalantinsk reported', Alma-Ata Kazakh radio network, 29 Aug. 1991, in *FBIS-SOV*-91-169, 30 Aug. 1991, p.126.
37. 'Testing testing', *The Economist*, 11 Apr. 1992, p.30; B. 'French finessse nuclear future', *Bulletin of the Atomic Scientists*, Se.1992, p.23; Butcher, M., Logan, C. and Plesch, D., 'French Nuclear Policy Since the Fall of the Wall', BASIC Report 93-1 (British American Security Information Council (BASIC): London, Feb 1993) p.28.
38. 'France proposes five-power test ban', *Washington Times*, 4 Nov. 1992, p.2; 'Paris seeks five-power N-weapons test talks', *Financial Times*, 4 Nov. 1992.
39. Drozdiak, W., 'Historic pact bans chemical weapons', *Washington Post*, 14 Jan. 1993, p.A24; Reuters, Paris, 'France to maintain nuclear test ban—Mitterand'. 13 Jan.1993.
40. BASIC Report (Note 62), p.27, note 37 *supra*.
41. *Le Monde*, 17 Dec.1993.
42. Xinhua News Agency, 12 Nov.1992, in Foreign Broadcast Information Service, Daily Report China (FBIS-CH). 12 Nov 1992, in IDDS, *Arms Control Reporter*, sheet 608. B 246, Nov.1992.
43. Crossette, B., 'Chinese set off their biggest explosion', *New*

York Times, 22 May 1992, P.A1; Vidale, J.E. and Benz, H.M. 'Seismological mapping of the structure near the base of the earth's mattle', Nature, 11 Feb. 1993, p.529. The Chineese explosion of 21 May 1992 consisted of one test of 660 kt. according to Vidale and Benz. See also IDDS. Arms_Control Reporter, sheet 608. B 236, July 1992.

44. 'First Supplementary List of Ratifications, Accessions, Withdrawals, etc. for 1992; presented to the British Parliament by the Secretary of State for Foreign and Commonwealth Affairs by Command of Her Majesty, Oct 1992 (Her Majesty's Stationery Office: London, October 1992), p.5.

45. *Trust and Verify*, Bulletin of the Verification Technology Informatiton Center (VERTIC), October 1993.

Chapter 5
Crafting a CTBT

In the background of all the developments stated in the preceding pages the current phase of comprehensive test ban negotiations began in full swing ever since the ball was set rolling on 10 August 1993, when the Conference on Disarmament gave its Ad Hoc Committee the "mandate to negotiate a comprehensive test ban."[1] The negotiations began in January 1994.

In addition to the mandate decision, papers were circulated by Mexico, Sweden, Australia, etc., giving different proposals, particularly on verification.[2] Simultaneously, in the General Assembly, on 10 November 1993, a draft resolution entitled 'Comprehensive Nuclear Test Ban Treaty' was submitted by 104 countries, and was sponsored by 53 additional countries. The draft was adopted as Resolution 48/70 on 16 December 1993.

CTBT negotiations opened in January 1994, stimulated by the end of the Cold War and then forthcoming NPT Review and Extension Conference. Non-aligned countries repeatedly called for a CTBT to be concluded by April 1995, while the nuclear-weapon states adamantly resisted any time-table. The G-21 concerns were twofold: they feared that once the NPT Conference was over, pressure for a CTBT within the P-5 (five permanent members of the United Nations, also the five nuclear-weapon states) governments would abate; and they were worried that changes of administration due in France in May 1995 and in USA and Russia in 1996 could scuttle the negotiations. Change of government in USA and UK had previously caused collapse of the tripartite test-ban negotiations during 1977-80. Despite attempts by the 1994 Chairman of the Nuclear Test Ban (NTB) Committee, Ambassador Miguel Marin Bosch of Mexico, to drive the CD towards early conclusion, some of the nuclear-weapon states wanted to ensure that there would be no possibility of finalizing the treaty before 1996 at the earliest. Although almost all the technical and political parameters for a CTBT were well known, the first year of negotiations nevertheless took some time in looking at the issue from first principles, before the process of negotiations gradually built up a draft text.

The 1994 NTB Committee Report, published in September, took the form of an 18-page summary of proceedings, followed by a 95-page appendix of text with alternative proposals and techniques in square brackets.[3] In addition to covering considerable technical ground, the first year of negotiations had seen states putting forward their 'wish' lists for what they would like to see in the treaty. Although the report took the form of a draft text for a CTBT, divided roughly into the articles that would be expected, it was laden with over a thousand pairs of brackets, indicating disputed language or ideas. While much of the language in brackets reflected minor differences of emphasis, drafting alternatives and punctuation, the political differences were far fewer, but with serious implications.[4]

Each of the nuclear-weapon states had a strategy for protecting its nuclear arsenal from the effects of a CTBT, reflected as bracketed language in the rolling text. France and UK wanted to be able to conduct safety tests "in exceptional circumstances". China demanded that nuclear explosions should be permitted for non-military purposes — the so-called peaceful nuclear explosions (PNE's) which had been tried for a while in the 1950s and 1960s by USA and Soviet Union for large-scale mining or construction, with little success. USA favoured a general scope for the treaty, without the exceptions for safety tests, but with a special agreement among the P-5 nuclear-weapon states that very small tests — {up to 4 lb. (1.8 kg)} — could be conducted. However, USA was pushing for an 'easy exit' clause in the treaty, whereby a state party could 'elect to withdraw from the treaty' at a review conference held ten years after entry into force. Fearing that it lacked the technology to conduct the low-yield 'hydronuclear tests' favoured by USA and UK, China insisted that the CTBT scope should prohibit any nuclear weapon test 'which releases nuclear energy'. Russia proposed a text that listed the prohibited environments, while at the same time it joined USA, UK and France in wanting to be able to conduct low-yield explosions, and had earlier expressed reservations about completely banning Peaceful Nuclear Explosions (PNE's). China seemed to want the treaty to do more than banning tests, requiring insertion of paragraphs and articles covering security assurances, 'no-first-use' and the peaceful uses of nuclear energy. Many of the brackets also reflected the interests of non-nuclear weapon states. Germany and Sweden wanted to ban preparations for testing, while Indonesia bracketed the word 'explosion', wanting all nuclear-weapon testing to be prohibited, whether explosive or not. There were a dozen different formulations for entry into force, ranging from a simple number to a strict requirement that all states with nuclear facilities should be on board before the CTBT is fully enforced. The technical discussions had piled detailed alternatives for monitoring techniques and insepections into the rolling text. The different requirements of an independent implementing organization or the International

Atomic Energy Agency (IAEA) also left a trail of text alternatives.

When the NTB Committee was convened on 3 February 1995, with Ambassador Ludiwk Dembinski (Poland) as its new Chairman, it was with the aim of converting this heavility bracketed 'rolling text' into a coherent comprehensive test ban treaty.

Structure of Negotiations

In accordance with the mandate, the NTB Committee had convened two working groups, Working Group (WG) 1 on Verification and Working Group 2 on Legal and Institutional Issues. In 1994 the NTB Committee had been chaired by Ambassador Marin Bosch of Mexico. Ambassador Wolfgang Hoffmann of Germany had chaired Working Group 1 and Ambassador Ludwik Dembinski of Poland had chaired Working Group 2.

In 1995, since it was the turn of the Group of Eastern European States, Ambassador Dembinski took the Chair of the NTB Committee. As before, two working groups(WG's) were established. Following a dispute within the Western group, during which France vetoed Australia's candidacy, Ambassador Jaap Ramaker of the Netherlands was made Chairman of WG 2 on Legal and Institutional Issues. With some of its key ambassadors due to leave the CD during the year, the G-21 had great difficulty in proposing someone to chair WG 2. To avoid delaying the start of the CTBT negotiations, they agreed to support Sweden, which had been a G-21 member until 1993 and had not joined the Western group, despite being a recent member of the European Union. During the year, WG 1, chaired by Ambassador Lars Norberg of Sweden, appointed seven 'Friends of the Chair' to focus negotiations on specific aspects of the verification regime. WG 2 appointed two 'Friends of the Chair', to consider questions relating to the implementing organization and entry into force (EIF).

The Rolling Text in 1995

Much of the work of 1995 consisted of clearing up the duplications, redundancies and inconsistencies in the rolling text, so that the political alternatives could be clearly seen. Work also proceeded throughout the year to determine the technologies and number of monitoring stations that would provide the most cost-effective coverage for detecting and identifying a clandestine nuclear test, wherever it might occur.

After several revisions, the rolling text contained in the September 1995 NTB Committee report consisted of 97 pages in two parts. Part I comprised the articles which were complete or nearly complete and provided for the following:

(i) Signature (open to all states);

(ii) Ratification (according to states' respective constitutional processes);

(iii) Accession (permitted after entry into force);

(iv) Depositary (Secretary-General of the United Nations);

(v) Status of the protocol(s) and annex(es) (integral to the Treaty);

(vi) Authentic texts (Arabic, Chinese, English, French, Russian and Spanish equally authentic);

(vii) National implementation measures (Responsibilities of states to have a 'national authority' to oversee implementation of the Treaty by its citizens and in its territories);

(viii) Measures to redress a situation and to ensure compliance, including sanctions (Procedures for dealing with non-compliance, including bringing any particularly serious case to the UN General Assembly and Security Council);

(ix) Settlement of disputes (Consultations between parties

or with the CTB Executive council, with arbitration by the International Court of Justice, if necessary);

(x) Privileges and immunities (for the Organisation and its staff);

(xi) Amendments (to be adopted only at an Amendment Conference, by a positive vote of a majority of parties, with no vote against).

Part II comprised those articles which were still heavily bracketed, indicating disagreements over the concept and language of the articles or, in some cases, opposition to the articles altogether. These included preamable, scope, peaceful use of nuclear energy, peaceful nuclear explosions, the organization, reservations, entry into force, duration and withdrawal, review of the treaty, security assurances for state parties, relation with other international agreements and verification.

On 23 January 1996, the first plenary session of the Conference on Disarmament agreed to the establishment of a nuclear test-ban committee. It began its work immediately under the chair of Jaap Ramaker of the Netherlands, reviewing the results of the intersessional work since September and making appointments of various chairs. By 26 January the Committee confirmed appointment of Grigori Berclennikerg of Russia as chair of Working Group 1 on verification and Mounir Zahran of Egypt as chair of Working Group 2 on Legal and Institutional Issue.

On 22 February 1996, Iran tabled a draft of CTBT text. Foreign minister Ali Akbar Vilayati told reporters that signatories would commit themselves to strive for "speediest possible achievement" of a n agreement on a time-bound framework.[5] On 29 February, Australia introduced another draft CTBT. In introducing it, Australia clarified that it was not an alternative to or substitute for the achievements which the Rolling Text represented.

China, India and Pakistan held that these texts were "purely personal" and could not circumvent the rolling text and the steady progress. USA was unhappy with several Australian suggestions. UK, France and Russia made positive noises about how both texts could help focus attention on key issues.

The first 1996 session of Conference on Disarmament ended on 28 March with Chair's working draft of a treaty. Most of the countries continued to set 30 June as the target date for completing a comprehensive test ban treaty.

Under pressure from China, India and Pakistan not to do anything which might prevent the Rolling text, Ramaker made clear that his "outline of a draft Comprehensive Nuclear Test Ban Treaty" was intended to provide "delegations and their capitals with a structured and manageable product of these negotiations so far, and highlight the major outstanding issues on which political decision-making is required."

Ramaker's working paper, structured as draft treaty, had a premable and 17 articles. Attached to it was a three-part protocol covering International monitoring system (IMS), on-site inspections and associated confidence building/ transparency measures, plus various annexes listing states and detailing the stations earmarked for inclusion in the IMS.

Four unnumbered articles appeared in brackets. These covered China's text proposal on peaceful uses of energy, peaceful nuclear explosions, security assurances for State Parties and the relations with other international agreements.[6]

Latest Developments

On 28 May 1996, exactly one month before the end of the second part of the CD's 1996 session, Ambassador

Jaap Ramaker presented his first draft text for a comprehensive nuclear test ban treaty (CTBT). Ramaker, Chair of the Nuclear Test Ban Committee emphasized that his completed text was not the final word, but intended to accelerate the pace of the negotiations that had been going on since 1994, and offer the negotiating countries the opportunity to reach final agreement on a CTBT before 28 June which was the target date set by the unopposed United Nations General Assembly (UNGA) resolution (50/65) in December 1995. On that date (28 June 1996) he submitted a slightly modified draft.

In contrast with his working paper delivered at the end of March, the Chair's draft text (CD/NTB/WP.330) contained no brackets or gaps. In choosing among different States' proposals, Ramaker had attempted to reflect as far as possible, options which could command the widest support. Consequently, this left a number of delegations disappointed. To reassure States holding strong positions, Ramaker stressed that his draft was to facilitate the last and final stage of negotiations, and that it had not been tabled with a "take it or leave it attitude".

India, Pakistan, Russia and China protested vigorously when Ramaker announced on 22 May, that he would shortly be tabling a draft treaty from the Chair. Munir Akram, Ambassador of Pakistan, warned that a "Treaty which descends from heaven or elsewhere may arrest rather than accelerate our negotiations and the fulfilment of our deadline." However, with most of other States holding the view that Ramaker could not have waited much longer if he wanted to conclude by 28 June, no-one called the draft `premature' when it was presented.

While there were mutterings that the draft represented the 'Western perspective', a number of Western countries, notably USA and UK, complained that the verification provisions leant too far towards the positions of G-21 group of non-aligned States. India raised particular objections pointing out that none of its positions had been incorporated in the draft, while other non-aligned countries pointed to provisions which they felt could provide some leverage to keep the nuclear-weapon States up to their obligations.[7]

Preamble

The preamble of the draft was intended to set the political context for the Treaty. In 1994, the preamable consisted of 18 hastily cobbled paragraphs, which had been reduced to 15 by 1995. Following China's decision on 5 September 1995 to accept the wording on the ultimate goal of eliminating nuclear weapons included in the 'Principles and Objectives', agreed to at the NPT Conference in May 1995, it dropped its insistence on commitment to "thorough nuclear disarmament" or the "complete prohibition and thorough destruction of nuclear arms at an early date" in two other paragraphs. This resulted in the dropping of paragraphs referring to the special responsibility of the nuclear-weapons states and to the need for further reductions of tactical and strategic nuclear weapons. However, India opposed any reference to the NPT, of which it was not a party, requesting the retention of other paragraphs on nuclear disarmament. China continued its demand for a paragraph urging conclusion of international agreements pledging not to use, or threaten to use, nuclear weapons against non-nuclear weapon states, nor to be the first to use nuclear weapons in any circumstance (no-first-use). This was opposed by the other four nuclear-weapon states. In addition to several paragraphs relating a test ban to further nuclear disarmament, the draft preamble referred to the 1963 PTBT, the preamble of the NPT, recent international agreements and cuts in nuclear arsenals and non-proliferation, as well as the need to make verification data publicly available. With India unlikely to accept direct references to the NPT, and most of the nuclear-weapon states refusing the wording that committed them 'too closely' to nuclear disarmament, it appeared that agreement would have to be based on some formulation developed from the 1995 Principles and Objectives,[8] but without direct dependence on the NPT.

Ramaker's text presented on 28 May 1996 portrayed a balance between the demands of non-nuclear weapon states seeking to set the political context of the treaty in disarmament background and that of the nuclear-weapon states opposing references to a time-bound framework. The Premable was specifically mentioned as an item for discussion in the reviews of the treaty. The key paragraph reads:

> "Convinced that the cessation of all nuclear weapon test explosions and all other nuclear explosions by constraining the development and qualitative improvement of nuclear weapons and ending development of advanced new types of nuclear weapons, constitutes an effective measure of nuclear disarmament and non-proliferation in all its aspects.[9]

The Preamble did not describe ending the qualitative improvement and development of nucler weapons as the "principle objective" of the treaty, a phrase strongly opposed by UK, nor does it include elimination of weapons "within a time bound framework" as demanded by India or references to the cessation of nuclear testing "within the framework of an effective nuclear diarmament process", another compromise sought by non-nucler weapon states.

The Preamble expressed the conviction that "the present international situation provides an opportunity to take further effective measures towards nuclear disarmament and against the proliferation of nuclear weapons in all its aspects" and declares the intention of States Parties to "take such measures." It also includes extract from the Australian model text, put forward in February 1996, stating that the CTBT: "will constitute a meaningful step in the realization of a systematic process to achieve nuclear disarmament."

The Preamble also reiterated the language from the NPT 'Principles and Objectives' stressing "the need for continued systematic and progressive efforts to reduce nuclear weapons globally, with the ultimate goal of eliminating those weapons, and of general and complete disarmament under strict and effective international control." This would for the first time commit non-NPT signatories such as India, Pakistan and Israel to this language and put the commitments made in NPT 'Principles and Objectives' in a legally binding document.

In response to demands from India, all direct references to the NPT and calls for NNW's to join the NPT have been removed. The treaty now welcomes "international agreements and other positive measures" on nuclear disarmament and prevention of nuclear proliferation and underlines the "importance of their full and prompt implementation." Description of recent reductions in arsenals of nuclear weapons as "deep" has been dropped.

China has dropped the demand for allowing peaceful nuclear explosions (PNE's), a position no other state supported. The Preamble includes language which clearly rules out PNE's. However, the article on 'Review of the Treaty', discussed below, provides a slight concession to the Chinese on this point. The Preamble also excludes language proposed by China urging the NWS's to conclude international agreements on 'no threat' or use of nuclear weapons against NNWS's or nuclear-weapon-free zones and on 'no-first-use' of nuclear weapons against each other. Ramaker's text of 28 June shows no modification of his draft of 28 May so far as the Preamble is concerned.

Scope

The scope is the backbone of the treaty, determining what shall be prohibited or permitted. While the working group debates exercised language options during much of 1994 and 1995, the real arguments centred on two issues, namely, so-called 'peaceful nuclear explosions' (PNE's) and 'activities not prohibited'. China advocated a ban on any nuclear weapon test explosion 'which releases nuclear energy' but wanted to be allowed to conduct nuclear explosions ostensibly for civil construction or commercial purposes. While Russia had flirted with the idea of PNE's, although its official position would support a ban, the other nuclear-weapon states and the vast majority (if not all) of non-nuclear weapon states want PNE's to be prohibited by the CTBT.

However, while arguing for 'comprehensive' scope language, most of the nuclear-weapon states discussed ways of not prohibiting very low-yield tests, called hydronuclear experiments (HNE). They argued that these tests would be useful in ensuring safety and reliability of the stockpiles, but critics apprehended that they could also assist in nuclear weapons development. Though all wanted some form of testing to continue, the P-5 were divided over the question how high a level to permit. USA, which in 1993 had fought an internal battle over 1 kt threshold, defined 'zero' as up to 4 lb (1.8 kg), i.e., a nuclear test which released nuclear energy up to the equivalent of 1.8 kg of TNT explosive power would not be regarded as a violation of a comprehensive test ban treaty. This was the yield defined for a 'one-point safety test.' Lacking the sophisticated equipment and techniques of USA, the others argued for higher threshold; UK, which uses American facilities at the Nevada Test Site, reportedly favoured a level of 40-50 kg; Russia wanted at least 10 tons; while France reportedly wanted 100-300 tons. China was also understood to be interested in permitting testing up to several hundred tons, although its representatives in the P-5 meetings were cagey about identifying numbers. China's official position, which opposed any fission yield, was primarily intended to obstruct agreement on a low threshold of a few kilograms, which it believed would solely benefit USA.

Going to Zero

During a debate on scope in WG2 in March, Australia presented a draft text on basic obligations:

1. Each State Party undertakes not to carry out any nuclear weapon test explosion or any other nuclear explosion, and to prohibit and prevent any such nuclear explosion at any place under its jurisdiction or control.

2. Each State Party undertakes, furthermore, to refrain from causing, encouraging, or in any way participating in the carrying out of any nuclear weapon test explosion or any other nuclear explosion."[10]

This is also the definition adopted by the draft of 28 June i.e., no change from the draft of 28 May.

Defining and Extending the Ban

Although the Australian text is now considered to be the front runner on the scope, it is not the only language that was considered. During the debate on the scope in WG2 on 27 June 1995, India and Indonesia both proposed drafts of text. The Indian text is discussed later. Indonesia's language, formalizing concerns raised last year, would prohibit all nuclear testing, whether explosive or not. Intended to cover laboratory activities such as computer simulation and inertial confinement fusion, this has little support, since most states consider that widening the scope to cover non-explosive testing of nuclear devices is not the purpose of a CTBT, however desirable it might be in terms of disarmament. There is additional concern that verification would be prohibitively intrusive and expensive.

In addition to China's language prohibiting any nuclear weapon test 'which releases nuclear energy' (in effect, a zero yield), two other 'scope' proposals were there to be resolved. The Russian text was based on the scope of the 1963 Partial Test Ban Treaty (PTBT), extending the list of prohibited environments to include underground tests. Opponents feared that this could conceal a loophole for contained explosions. Germany and Sweden till very late preferred the general prohibition to include 'preparing to test'. As the France-US-UK decisions dissipated the anxious speculation about thresholds, pressure grew on those countries with alternative proposals to drop them in favour of the Australian text, with the understanding that it meant a zero-yield treaty with no exceptions or threshold.

Peaceful Nuclear Explosions (PNE's)

Two disputed texts related to China's desire to retain the right to conduct nuclear explosions 'purely for scientific research or civilian applications'. One dealt specifically with PNE's, setting out the conditions for preparing and conducting the explosions, and the other underlines the 'inalienable right' of State Parties to nuclear energy for non-military purposes. Although Russia very early on expressed a desire to keep open an option for PNE's, the Russian delegation made clear that they would not hold up consensus on the issue.

The vast majority of states wanted a CTBT to ban all nuclear explosions, and would not accept a treaty with any provision for PNE's. China's demand for PNE's was worrying many negotiators who feared that China's real strategy might be to hold up negotiations until it was too late to conclude in 1996, in the hope that elections in USA would deliver a Republican administration opposed to a CTBT. In that case USA, not China, would be blamed for failure to conclude the treaty.

In the CD plenary on 23 January 1996, Pakistan argued for a scope with "no exceptions for any reason". It said concepts such as zero-yield or no-yield "must be compatible with the CTBT's fundamental aims." [11]

The Chinese delegate on 26 January 1996, rejected the phrase, "any other nuclear explosion" in the 'scope' text because of the PNE's and "because of our belief that micro-nuclear explosions such as inertial confinement fusion (ICF) have wide prospect of application in the field of nuclear energy." [12] Till January 1996 Russia had not endorsed Australian definition on scope.

On February 1, the Egyptian delegate said that the ban should include all tests. The Sri Lankan delegate also speaking at the plenary said, "having banned nuclear weapon test explosions and other nuclear explosions, should we permit sub-critical tests which would allow the nuclear weapon states to improve their arsenals and design third generation nuclear weapons?" Chile also called for total ban including PNE's. [13]

By this time most delegations had come round to supporting the Australian text. China sought to permit PNE's. South Africa proposed that the Australian scope be understood to recognize the evidence that test preparations would be admissible. Australia warned against over extension of scope and Japan said that it would be a tragedy if there was no treaty because of each state insisting on a treaty incorporating its national concern. Indonesia withdrew its proposal (discussed earlier) in favour of Australian text for it understood that the latter banned all types of nuclear tests in all environments for all times.

Iran had worried many by adopting a 'general

obligation' that reverts back to the prohibition on 'any nuclear weapon test and any other nuclear explosion' which Indonesia withdrew earlier in February, and used part of the Russian formula by which the prohibition would cover only areas under a state's jurisdiction and control, leaving a grey area. According to Iran's text:

1. Each state party undertakes to prohibit, to prevent and not to carry out, any nuclear weapon test or any other nuclear explosion at any place under its jurisdiction or control.

2. Each state party undertakes, furthermore, to refrain from causing, encouraging, or in any way participating in the carrying out of any nuclear weapon test or any other nuclear explosion referred to in paragraph 1 of this Article.

The Ramaker text of May 28 retained the formulation originally proposed by Australia in March 1995. France, USA, UK and recently Russia had all given their support to "zero-yield" formulation.

The Chinese gave up their demand for PNE's. On 14 May 1996 the Chinese Ambassador Sha Zukang, said that China, "still supports the idea of PNE's under strict international supervision, but, Beijing is prepared to be flexible on the issue."

On June 6, the Chinese told the conference that it would temporarily give up its demand for the right to conduct "peaceful" nuclear explosions if other countries agreed to reexamine the issue in the future — at the review conference. The Ramaker draft of 28 June 1996 has provisions for Review Conference to consider PNE's. If the conference decides that PNE's may be permitted, the treaty will be so amended.

Egypt has reiterated its support for the proposal put forward by Indonesia in 1995, demanding deletion of "explosion" from first part, so that the treaty would ban all nuclear-weapon tests and any nuclear explosion. This is a demand supported by India.

The nuclear-weapon states made it clear that they regard 'zero-yield' as a major concession and would not go further on 'scope'.

Closure of the Test Sites

Closure and clean up of the test sites, including their restoration to original inhabitants, where appropriate, have long been demanded by CTBT campaigners, on human rights and environmental principles, as well as to prevent further nuclear testing. The Soviet test site at Semipalatinsk is now under the control of the independent Republic of Kazakhstan; the remaining Russian test sites are on the Arctic island of Novaya Zemlya, formerly the home of the indigenous Nenets people. The Maohi people of Tahiti-Polynesia have long demanded restoration of the coral atolls of Moruroa and Fangataufa used by France for nuclear testing in the South Pacific. Native Americans of the Western Shoshone have been at the forefront of campaigns to bring to halt the testing by USA and UK at the Nevada site, part of their ancestral lands validated by the Ruby Valley Treaty of 1963. At different times during the past two years, Algeria, Iran, India, Indonesia, Nigeria and Pakistan have called for the test sites to be closed, although this has not been discussed under 'scope'. The nuclear-weapon states argue that the test sites are also research laboratories and that they have to maintain a 'prepared-ness to test' as insurance and deterrence against any break-out. Given their determined opposition, closure would not seem feasible at this time. However, if hydronuclear experiments have now been ruled out, there could be some intermediate stage of mothballing or dismantling facilities specifically associated with nuclear testing, combined with confidence-building measures, for example, notification of non-prohibited activities such as drilling or mining at, or near, the former test sites.

The Implementing Organization

The 1994 rolling text on the implementing organization was a mass of conflicting brackets. For a very long time no decision had been taken on the question whether the implementation and verification of the CTBT should be entrusted to the International Atomic Energy Agency (IAEA), as proposed by Sweden, but supported only by Brazil and Egypt, or to a separate organization. The 1995 rolling text proposed an independent CTB-specific organization, based in Vienna, with some sharing or leasing of IAEA facilities and expertise. Some delegations had raised questions about the high cost of telecommunications in Austria, given the importance of on-line data transmission, and others wanted more information on what Austria was prepared to provide to CTBT Organization, before deciding. Vienna is so far the sole candidate for hosting the Organization.

After a long debate, negotiators decided on the name 'Comprehensive Nuclear Test-Ban Treaty Organization'. It is sought to comprise a Conference of State Parties, an Executive Council of 51 members, and a Technical Secretariat which would carry out the verification measures and coordinate the international monitoring system (IMS). In the rolling text this provision was in brackets, the text was then considerably tidied up so that the alternatives are more clearly defined. This was accomplished by the 'Friend of the Chair on Organization', Ajit Kumar of India, and his team from Canada, Cuba and India.

The CTBT Organization as envisaged in both the May 28 and June 28 1996 texts is distinct from the IAEA. Its (central) decisions will be concerned with the structure, composition and function of its bodies, particularly the Executive Council. The Conference of

State Parties would comprise all State Parties, each with one vote. As the principle decision-making body, it would elect (or designate) the members of the Executive Council, appoint the Director-General of the Technical Secretariat, decide on funding and rules of procedure, oversee the verification regime, and ensure compliance with the treaty.

Executive Council

Since the meeting of the Conference of State Parties would be a major (and expensive) undertaking, the more immediate decision-making would be entrusted to an Executive Council. The P-5 nuclear-weapon states wanted to ensure that they have seats on the Executive Council, but many others rejected the concept of permanent seats. The Ramaker text of June 28 envisages 51 members in the Executive Council based on "equitable geographical distribution."

Organization

The CTBTO, according to the Ramaker text of 28 May 1996 as well as 28 June 1996, will be located in Vienna and will compose of Conference of State Parties, Executive Council and Technical Secretariat headed by Director General. It will be independent but is expected to make use of expertise and facilities available with the IAEA. Ramaker had opted for a 51-member Executive Council with seats elected and designated from six geographical regions, ensuring continuous membership for those with high stake in terms of nuclear capability and funding of the Organization. Alphabatic rotation of one seat per region will ensure that no state is excluded.

Verification

The purpose of the verification regime is to provide sufficient confidence in the Organization's ability to detect a clandestine test, and to ensure that any state or sub-national group would realize that the costs of cheating and the risks of detection would be too high.

The CTBT verification regime is envisaged to comprise an international monitoring system (IMS), the core of which would be a global seismic network; consultations and information exchange; and on-site inspections. Most of the states consider that transparency and confidence-building measures could play an important part. Others want the international verification regime to be supplemented, where appropriate, by information derived from national technical means (NTM). Russia, in particular, has long advocated using NTM to supplement the IMS in order to keep costs down while maintaining a highly deterrent verification capability. Any incorporation of NTM is strongly opposed by China and Pakistan. Though many G-21 countries have reservations, fearing that NTM could be employed in a discriminatory manner, others have expressed interest in suggestions made by France and others for allowing NTM data but according it a lesser weight than information gained through the international system.

On-Site Inspections (OSI)

Negotiations on on-site inspections are emerging as a battleground for fundamentally different political approaches to verification, confidence and security. Anxious to protect military and commercial secrets, governments want to prevent unnecessary intrusion. At the same time, they acknowledge that a physical inspection is sometimes the only way to remove suspicions if the monitoring system detects an anomalous event. It will be necessary to balance the requirements of inspections, national security and international confidence.

Outstanding issues include: the procedures for consultation and clarification; the origins, basis and timing of an OSI request; evaluation of information related to an inspection request; the decision-making process for undertaking an inspection; and whether OSI should be a single or multi-phased operation. Details about composition of inspection teams, managed access, rights and responsibilities have yet to be determined, but would be expected to fall into place if the major political differences can be resolved.

Following consultations, the 'Friend of the Chair' on trigger mechanisms, Dr. Klaus Arnhold of Germany, reported the view that OSI should be a rare event, carried out in the most timely, least intrusive and most cost-effective manner possible. The OSI regime should deter from abusive or frivolous inspections. Typically, inspections could include routine inspections, challenge inspections (where little notice is given), and observation of notified activities such as large chemical explosions. Most states argue against routine inspections in this treaty. Some states object to the concept of challenge inspections, fearing that they could be used to convey distrust or suspicion, even when not undertaken in response to a suspicious event. Many states advocate transparency and procedures for consultation and clarification, arguing that this should relieve the necessity for OSI's in most cases. Key factors for consideration are timeliness and security. Mechanisms for deciding whether to conduct an OSI must be fast enough to ensure that essential evidence is not lost or erased, while providing an adequate screen to prevent abusive or improper inspections. China, Israel, India and Pakistan have argued for OSI to be regarded as a tool of last resort, only undertaken if a mandatory and stringent process of consultation has failed to resolve doubts. Russia too argues that a request for inspection should only be made after all other possibilities for clarifying the situation have been exhausted. USA, France, UK and most Western states put greater emphasis on quick access and the prompt gathering of vital evidence.

In December 1994, the Group of Experts on On-Site Inspection reported on the phenomena associated with nuclear explosions in particular environments (CD/NTB/WP 198). Focussing on underground explosions, they argued that venting of radioactive gases, particularly xenon, and aftershocks in the vicinity of the explosion were tell-tale signs that would vanish if not observed within one month, and preferably during the first weeks. They also identified roads, debris or tailings, the traces of which might be erased or concealed, arguing that evidence on these too should be sought as soon as possible.

The report identified other manifestations which were less time-critical, some of which could only be verified by drilling and with sophisticated instruments for detection and measurement. These include: surface cratering, evidence of an underground cavity or rubble zone, surface changes from ground spallation, residual underground radioactivity, the presence of radioactive argon-37 gas, changes in groundwater level, and anomalies of heat, pressure and gas flow indicating a fractured geology.

In response to this report, USA in February 1995 proposed that OSI should be conducted in two phases. The first would be of relatively short duration and low intrusiveness, but would have to be conducted soon after detection of a suspicious event. It could include aerial overflights and visual inspections, measurement of radioactivity, and seismological measuresments. The second phase would be more intrusive and of longer duration, involving expensive drilling. USA argued that besides ensuring early collection of evidence, this would keep costs down, since the first phase could well satisfy the concerns of the requesting party and Technical

Secretariat. To intiate the first phase quickly, USA had argued for a simpler process for deciding to proceed, with a 'red-light' agreement, meaning that the inspection would go ahead on the basis of a request from a State Party unless the Executive Council decides against it. By contrast, the second phase should go ahead only if the Executive Council agrees by positive vote (a 'green light' decision). China also backs the two-phase approach, and proposes a time-line that could make this possible within the first three weeks. Though France would accept a two-phase OSI concept, the other nuclear-weapon states are reportedly unconvinced. In September 1995 Pakistan suggested that the 'time-critical' evidence from aftershocks and noble gas releases was exaggerated, and would be 'extremely low' for a well camouflaged test. Pakistan's Ambassador Munir Akram counselled against conducting OSI in a "hasty manner".

For the purposes "of ensuring the fairness, objectivity and effectiveness of CTBT verification", China and Pakistan argue for requests and decisions to be based solely on IMS data. The other nuclear-weapon states, Western and Eastern European countries, envisage some incorporatin of information derived from national technical means. In a statement on 30 June 1995, the G-21 stated the view that "the judgement by the Organization (regarding OSI) should be based on data received from the IMS" and that "it should be exclusive responsibility of the Organization to carry out on-site inspection in areas both within and beyond the jursidiction or control of State Parties."

In August 1995, France put forward a proposal that OSI could be requested on the basis of IMS or national information, but with different decision-making procedures and weight accorded to each. In effect, the French proposal was for a 'red light' decision for an OSI based on IMS data, and the more stringent 'green light' process if the request depended on NTM data. That means that an OSI would automatically proceed if the Technical Secretariat deemed IMS data to be sufficient, unless a two-thirds majority of the Executive Council specifically voted to prevent the inspection. A request based on national data would require a positive decision from the Executive Council to proceed. As several states, including some non-aligned states, expressed cautious interest, China on 5 September 1995 flatly rejected any incorporation of NTM data, a position reinforced by Pakistan the following week.

Some states have expressed concern that China's positions on verification on NTM and on-site inspections are contradictory. If China is worried about frivolous, unfounded or abusive inspections, supplementing IMS data with information from other sources, including national means, would help clarify an ambiguous event, thereby reducing the likelihood of an OSI. Similarly, the reasons China provides for wanting a satellite network and EMP sensors to monitor for signs of atmospheric or upper-atmospheric testing would be met for a fraction of the cost if evidence from intelligence and commerical satellites were admitted. Rather than rejecting NTM out of hand, it might be better to construct modalities that would allow the verification regime to benefit from national data, while minimizing the opportunities for biased or selective utilization. The modalities could provide for equal access and impartial evaluation of such data when it is included as evidence in a request for OSI. Whether used officially in the verification regime or not, national intelligence and NTM, especially of the more technologically advanced states, will continue to monitor the world. Arguing against NTM and for a fully defined international regime for a treaty such as the CTBT will not succeed in making this level of intelligence available to all states, but could fatally delay the treaty's conclusion or make it too expensive for many states to ratify. In the interests of the developing and less affluent states, it could be more constructive to define the terms under which such additional monitoring data may be used or rejected.

By February 1996 several states including China, Pakistan and Israel wanted the period of consultation and clarification to be obligatory. Russia argued that the duration and requirements for consultation should remain flexible. France, Britain and USA and most of the Western states called for speedy OSI to catch time-critical phenomenon such as aftershock and noble gas releases. In general the West and East European states held that an OSI request could be based on any relevant information.[14] Indonesia, Nigeria and Algeria argued that only IMS information should trigger inspections.

While there are some structural differences between the two drafts, the main OSI issues for the negotiations are: what kind of information can back an OSI request; and what kind of decision-making procedure gives the go ahead. Both the Iranian and Australian drafts had a presumption of access, with two phases for OSI: essentially 'red light' (go ahead unless a two-thirds majority (Australia) or three-fourths majority (Iran)of the EC decide against it) for the first time-critical phase which should consist of visual inspection, overflights, closer monitoring, etc; and 'green light' (requiring a two-thirds majority of the EC) for the more intrusive second phase.

Australia adopted French proposal that the first phase of OSI would be 'red light' if based on IMS data but 'green' if based solely on NTM. Australia allowed OSI requests to be based on data from the IMS and/or by the elements of the treaty verification regime, whereas for Iran, an OSI request must be based only on IMS data. However, Iran does not entirely slam the door shut on NTM, allowing supplementary information to be provided to the Technical Secretariat. Nevertheless, the key difference was that the Australian text would allow an OSI request to be based on any relevant information, while the Iran OSI request should have been backed only by IMS information. Under 'associated measures' Australia had clauses encouraging "access by all State Parties to other technical information and data relevant to the verification of the basic obligations..." and elsewhere tries to provide mechanisms for sharing NTM data to meet some of the non-aligned group's objections that it is discriminatory *per se.* On March 26, Finland supported a two-phase OSI with 'red light' being automatic for the early phase.

By the time the CD winter session ended (28 March 1996) the Russians were saying that if their proposal for monitoring stations to be placed at the test site ws not accepted, the Duma would reject the treaty, since Novaya Zehua would be unfairly monitored to a higher degree than Nevada and Lop Nor. China, on the other hand, characterized any further enhancement of the detection level as "excessive and unacceptable". It argued that Lop Nor was monitored to an intensity higher than the global average.

The Ramaker text of 28 May 1996 says, "the on-site inspection request shall be based on information collected by International Monitoring System, or any relevant technical information obtained by national technical means of verification in a manner consistent with generally recognized principles of international law or on a combination thereof." [15] This is repeated in the Ramaker text of 28 June 1996. The Ramaker text of 28 May stated that the inspection team would submit its report 30 days after the approval of OSI. This period has been reduced to 25 days in the 28 June draft.

The inclusion of the phrase "international law" was intended to address the concerns of countries like China and other non-aligned countries about use of NTM while still allowing it. Thus, while the Chinese agreed for limited use of NTM for requesting OSI, they said (on 7 June 1996) that the data must be technical, reliable, verifiable and obtained in consistence with the China-accepted principles of international law. The Chinese delegation was categorically against triggering OSI with the so-called "human intelligence". OSI could only be the last resort of the verification system to be used "under extreme circumstances."[16] The Ramaker text of 28 June says that no state "shall have to accept simultaneous inspections" on its territory.

Ramaker provided some conditions that NTM would not be used in an "unqualified manner". The Ramaker text of 28 May says that even state party shall have the right to use information from NTM; the 28 June text says that no state shall be precluded from using information from NTM. He repudiated the argument of USA that an inspection should proceed automatically unless the Executive Council deliberately votes against it by a simple majority of the Council.[17]

In CD plenary of January 1996, China continued to support monitoring using optical sensors on satellites and EMP ground-based stations. USA opposed the satellite system because of the expense; even though it continued to operate its Vela system of optional monitor on satellites, USA stated, "We would definitely not turn it over to the IMS".

As for EMP monitoring, because the stations could pick up line of atmospheric explosions, a network would require many EMP stations. Though individually such stations cost relatively little, in the aggregate an EMP network would cost a great deal of money.[18] USA believed infrasound monitors would do the same job better and cheaper.

Pakistan continued to voice opposition to NTM initiating an OSI and its support of the 'green light' procedure. Russia proposed that each testing site should receive a seismic monitoring station and a radiation monitoring station. This would level the monitoring conditions and not cause an increase in the cost of the verification system.[19] Russia said that the the instruments at test site were added because its perception of IMS requirements had changed with the move to zero-yield. The presence of these new stations would increase sensitivity of monitoring at Nevada, Lop Nor and Novaya Zemlya. China's reaction was extremely strong; others were ready to consider it, although a number of states criticized Russia for not raising the issue before the seismic network had been agreed to on 8 February 1995. Algeria argued that what could not be verified "should not be referred to for the time-being, without being explicitly or implicitly set aside, at the CD plenary."[20]

Both the Australian and Iranian drafts endorse the IMS based on the four technologies (seismic, hydroacoustic, infrasound and radionucleide) and find different solutions for keeping the possibility of incorporating satellite and EMP data in future, neither explictly backing nor ruling out such networks as part of the IMS or supplementary data (using commercial data, for example). Although Iran's Foreign Minister said that Iran supported the Russian proposal for monitoring stations at the actual test sites, a reading of the lists provided by Iran and Australia revealed that both the lists seemed to be identical (and the same as the latest update for the rolling text). Iran acknowledged this and said "they would prefer them on the test site" but regarded it as too complicated to identify the relocations, whatever it means!

Iran did not explicitly advocate closure of the test sites in its text, although again, Velayati spoke for this. Rather, Iran proposed that "the State Parties shall cease all activities related to nuclear testing and close those parts related to the testing in the site. The State Parties shall also ensure that specifically designed equipment for testing shall be destroyed." Iran also wants declaration of information from past tests including dates and yields and so on.

Speaking on 7 March 1996 at the CD, the Russian delegate called for identical transparency for all nuclear test sites to be accompanied with improvement in the seismological and radionucleide subsystem of IMS. He advocated use of NTM "in accordance with universally recognized principles of international law," a phrase denoting inadmissibility of certain kinds of spying. Cuba also opposed the use of NTM.[21]

On 19 March 1996, a progress report on GSETT-3 was submitted. The ad hoc group of scientific experts noted that the first year of the experiment had demonstrated the feasibility of an IMS and the achievement of the expected capabilities. By the end of 1995, the network comprised 41 primary stations and 76 auxiliary stations which provided a worldwide mean of 90 per cent detection at Mb4-4.2, which improved to Mb 3.6 in areas covered more densely. Only 18 per cent of the events could be located within 1,000 square kilometres. "Thus the detection and location capabilities observed so far are of an untenned and non-calibrated system."[22] China and Pakistan continued vehement criticism of NTM.

Rejecting the use of NTM, Pakistani Foreign Minister Sardar Aseef Ali said on 28 March, "We should not countenance any mechanism which by-passes the political and technical role of CTBTO." The Chinese delegate Sha Zukang said, "It is necessary to prevent certain countries from taking advantage of their superior NTM to frequently harass and discredit developing countries with dubious information and even infringe upon ligitimate security interests of the latter."

Supporting the 'green-light' procedure before each phase of OSI, the Chinese delegate said, "it is inappropriate to prejudge the inspected state as 'violator' before the inspection result is endorsed by EC."

By the time the winter session of CD ended the position was: USA said that it could not get the CTBT ratified if national sources of intelligence were excluded from verification regime. China, India and Pakistan ruled it out, arguing for verification to be based on IMS data solely. They said that any incorporation of it would be discriminatory.

Speaking on 23 May 1996 at CD, the British Minister for Foreign Office, David Davis, said that parties should be able to bring all relevant information to bear on the verification process. "No artificial distinctions should be drawn, and no source of data be excluded", he added.

Softening its stand on NTM a little, the Chinese Ambassador to CD, Sha Zukang said, "If NTM were to be used as a basis for requesting OSI, they must be technical, verifiable and obtained in consistence with international law." The Chinese felt that the problem with NTM was that these differed from country to country since all countries were at different levels of development.[23]

Entry into Force

The text on entry into force has been substantially cleaned of redundancies, but there has been little further progress on agreeing to the conditions under which the treaty will come into effect. Most states want to ensure that the P-5 and nuclear threshold states will be on board when the CTBT enters into force, but want to avoid imposing terms so strict that the treaty can be held hostage by one or a few states. Depending on whether negotiators favoured a simple numerical option or a specific group of states, the choice comes down to a number, a list and/or a mechanism.

A simple number, such as 60, is favoured by those who want to ensure early entry into force. Earlier, for for USA and several other states, ratification by all five declared NWS's was a minimal condition. Russia proposed the IAEA list of states with nuclear research programmes or power reactors — about 60, including all threshold states. For the same reason France and UK had favoured entry into force following ratification by all members of the expanded CD. Although prepared to support the IAEA list if CD expansion was not accomplished, they pointed out that threshold states which had been involved in CTBT negotiations would be less likely to obstruct entry Into force (EIF) than if they were specified only because of their technological capability. China has now dropped this requirement in favour of the IAEA list. The principal drawback of a list is that entry into force could be delayed by any particular state withholding its ratification, thereby, in effect, exercising a veto.

To avoid the treaty being held hostage and enable the verification regime to be implemented, some states have proposed combining a list with a formula for exercising a waiver. Two waiver proposals were considered in 1995, and appeared in brackets in the rolling text. One, advocated by Australia, was based on the 1967 Tlateloco Treaty, which specified conditions for entry into force, but gave the right to each of the parties to waive the requirements, thereby allowing the treaty to enter into force individually. Combined with a specific list, this would have to include some mechanism for a sufficient number of states to decide to inaugurate the verification system, or else implementation would have to be based on national monitoring, thereby undermining some of the rationale for a multilateral CTBT.

The US waiver proposal calls for a conference of

states which have ratified, two years after signature, provided all the P-5 have ratified. The conference participants could then decide whether to waive the specific EIF requirements, to let the treaty enter into force for them, including inaugurating the verification regime. While acknowledging the importance of accession by all the nuclear-weapon states, several states from all groupings were unhappy with the US waiver proposal, for, it provided too big an opportunity for veto. In particular, they cited uncertainty about China's intentions, since China promised only to cease testing "once a CTBT has entered into force', and not upon signatures, as is the usual expectation, according to common practice and the Vienna Convention on the Law of Treaties. While finding the idea of waiver conference interesting in principle, they suggested that only a timing condition be placed, i.e., a conference could be convened by decision of a majority of those which had ratified two years after signature. Some had even suggested that while all could attend as observers, only those which had ratified could participate in taking the decisions. This, it was felt, could exert pressure on the recalcitrant states in a variety of ways, the most important of which might be loss of influence and appointments in the CTBT Organisation at an early stage.

On 26 January 1996 India introduced a working paper saying, "This Treaty shall enter into force after all State Parties have committed themselves to the attainment of the goal of total elimination of nuclear weapons within a well-defined time framework of 10 years." China sought a lengthy EIF procedure, according to which the treaty would take effect one year after a number of requirements, including the treaty remaining open for signatures for a minimum of two years.[24]

Since China said that it would end testing only on entry into force, some believed that any proposal requiring ratification by nuclear-weapon states would put a veto into the hands of China.

Both models provided innovative attempts to resolve the central problem of EIF: how to ensure the P-5 plus 3 without giving them veto power. Australia advocated all CD plus observes (now some 75 states, including all the awkward ones), with a waiver conference after two years called by all those who have ratified (a modified version of the US proposal from last year, but without the US condition of all P-5 on board). Iran provided the IAEA list of 68 states which have or have had nuclear capability, and specified EIF if 65 out of these 68 states ratified (a modified version of the percentage option). Australia emphasized that its national preference was still for a simple number, adding that this proposal was an attempt to provide a creative solution to the current deadlock.

By the time the winter CD session came to an end (28 March 1996), UK floated an EIF formula which targeted only the eight—five nuclear and three threshold nuclear states. While Pakistan accepted this proposal, India was unhappy that the formula discriminated against it. South Africa and others objected that it set an unhealthy principle by appearing to confer special status on threshold states.

On entry into force, the Ramaker text of 28 May 1996 discarded all previous formulations in favour of a new approach based on the practical requirements of the treaty's verification regime. Article XIV specifies that the treaty would enter into force 180 days after instruments of ratification have been deposited by all states which have seismological stations comprising the primary network for verification and all states which have radionucleide laboratories. This is a total of 37 states listed in the protocol to the treaty and includes all five NWS's and the three 'threshold' states — India, Pakistan and Israel.

This was the original UK demand although the US representative to CD said on 23 May 1996 that UK did not hold this position so firmly "because we can have no interest in seeing the negotiations fail". *The Washington Post* in a report on 18 June 1996 quoted the US officials as saying that Washington would join other four declared nuclear powers in pressing the three countries — India, Pakistan and Israel to accept the ban. Speaking on 23 May 1996, the Pakistani representative Munir Akram reiterated his earlier stand that unless each of eight states signed and ratifed a test ban would not be comprehensive and sustainable.

In its statement to CD on 6 June 1996, China said, "For the sake of nuclear non-proliferation it was essential to condition entry into force of the treaty on the joining by all those states that were capable of conducting nuclear explosions." The Chinese delegation was against any proposal that might weaken this principle, such as the waiver clause.

Ramaker compromise proved to be controversial. While avoiding the difficulties of singling out the eight nuclear and 'threshold' states, it also made the treaty hostage to ratification by 37 states. After India's request to take its monitoring facilities out, in the 28 June 1996 draft of Ramaker, entry into force has been made conditional on ratification by states having research and power reactors. The list is based on IAEA assessment and includes India.

Review of the Treaty

Following the retraction in January 1995 of the US proposal for a special right of withdrawal after ten years, dubbed the 'easy exit' clause, general agreement was reached on providing for a review conference after ten years, with further ten year reviews if a majority of states so desired. Some states, however, questioned whether any formal review process was necessary in this treaty. They considered that the issue could be addressed more appropriately in the section on the Conference of State Parties in the Organisation, with review of the treaty being an ongoing function of the Conference.

Article VIII on 'Review', in the Ramaker text of 28 May 1996 specified that the review conference of State Parties to the treaty would "review the operation and effectiveness of the Treaty, including its Preamble with a view to ensuring that its objects and purposes are being realized. Such review shall take into account any new scientific and technological developments relevant to the treaty."[25]

There had been some discussions mentioning PNE's in the 'Amendment' section of the draft treaty. However, because of strong opposition from several countries, particularly Canada, specific mention of PNE's was omitted entirely in the 28 May draft. As stated earlier, provision for PNE's during Review has been made.

Duration and Withdrawal

The treaty is intended to be of unlimited duration, with the standard article permitting withdrawal if a state decideds that "extraordinary events... have jeopardised its supreme national interests". Pakistan has suggested that a nuclear test conducted by another country, whether party to the treaty or not, could be sufficient reason for withdrawal. The rolling text also carries a bracketed clarification relating `extraordinary events' to the violation of the spirit, object and/or purpose of the treaty. This provision has remained unchanged in the 28 June Ramaker text.

The draft text of the comprehensive Test Ban Treaty contained in the working paper CD/NTP/WP 330/Rev.1 has been aptly summarised in the July issue of Trust and Verify. The relevant portions of this article by article summary read as:

Preamble

The Preamble, where the intentions of the Parties to the Treaty are expressed, contains such paragraphs as:

Stressing therefore the need for continued systematic and progressive efforts to reduce nuclear weapons globally, with the ultimate goal of eliminating those weapons, and of general and complete disarmament under strict and effective international control.

Recognizing that the cessation of all nuclear weapon test explosions and all other nuclear explosions, by constraining the development and qualitative improvement of nuclear weapons and ending the development of advanced new types of nuclear weapons, constitutes an effective measure of nuclear disarmament and non-proliferation in all its aspects.

Further recognizing that an end to all such nuclear explosions will thus constitute a meaningful step in the realization of a systematic process to achieve nuclear disarmament.

Noting also the views expressed that this Treaty could contribute to the protection of the environment.

Article I — Basic Obligations

Article 1 reads as follows:

1. Each State Party undertakes not to carry out any nuclear weapon test explosion or any other nuclear explosion, and to prohibit and prevent any such nuclear explosion at any place under its jurisdiction or control.
2. Each State Party undertakes, furthermore, to refrain

from causing, encouraging, or in any way participating in the carrying out of any nuclear weapon test explosion or any other nuclear explosion.

This text is understood to include all text explosions down to a zero yield.

Peaceful nuclear explosions, which were the subject of much discussion before a scope text could be agreed, are now referred to in Article VIII (Review of the Treaty).

Article II - The Organisation

This establishes the 'Comprehensive Nuclear Test-Ban Treaty Organization'(CTBT or 'the Organization'). The CTBTO is to be based in Vienna and though an independent body 'shall seek to utilise expertise and facilities, as appropriate, and to maximise cost efficiencies, through co-operative arrangements with other international organizations such as the International Atomic Energy Agency'.

The CTBTO will have a Conference of the States Parties, an Executive Council and a Technical Secretariat. The Technical Secretariat will contain the International Data Centre (IDC) and will operate the International Monitoring System (IMS).

The Conference of the State Parties will meet annually, or in special session if the circumstances so require.

In the CTBTO the Executive Council will have 51 members. The allocation of states to regional groups for the purposes of allocating seats at the Executive Council is specified and contained in Annex 1 to the Treaty. The groups are: Africa; Eastern Europe; Latin America and the Caribbean; Middle East and South Asia; North America and Western Europe; and South East Asia, the Pacific and the Far East. Israel is included as a member of the Middle East and South Asia group which has prompted dissent from Iran.

Article III - National Implementation Measures

Article III obliges States Parties to prohibit natural and legal persons that it has control over from carrying out any activity prohibited to a State Party under the Treaty.

Article IV - Verification

The verification system is based on multinational data collected by the International Monitoring System and collated at the International Data Centre. Data collected by 'national technical means' (i.e., national intelligence assets) may be used to back up a call for an on-site inspection if it has been obtained 'in a manner consistent with generally recognized principles of international law'. This is understood to exclude human intelligence for espionage purposes.

Monitoring technologies

The International Monitoring System is based on four monitoring technologies, specified in the Protocol; seismological, radionuclide, hydrocoustic and infrasound, These are set out in the Protocol to the Treaty (see below)

On-Site inspection - decision making

The text states that:

The decision to approve the on-site inspection shall be made by a majority of all members of the Executive Council. (Article IV, paragraph 46).

Some states, in particular china and Pakistan, had called for this decision to be made by a two-thirds majority — thus requiring 34 votes instead of 26. (China is now ready to reduce it to 30 from 34).

On-site inspection - limits of powers

Article IV, paragraph 57(c) reads that a State Party

subject to an inspection shall have the obligation 'to provide access within the inspection area for the sole purpose of determining facts relevant to the purpose of the inspection, taking into account national security and confidentiality concerns) and any constitutional obligations it may have with regard to proprietary rights or searches and seizures.'

Article V - Measures to Redress a Situation and to Ensure Compliance, Including Sanctions

This Article gives powers to the Conference of the States Parties, in the event of questions of non-compliance with the Treaty: to suspend a State Party from exercising rights and privileges under the Treaty; to recommend collective measures; or to bring a case to the attention of the United Nations.

Article VI - Settlement of Disputes

This Article allows organs of the CTBTO and the International Court of Justice (World Court) to assist in settlement of disputes between States Parties on issues relating to the Treaty.

Article VII - Amendments

Any amendment would have to be agreed by consensus at an Amendment Conference.

Article VIIII - Review of the Treaty

Article VIII allows for review conferences to be held every ten years if the Conference of the States Parties so decides in the preceding year. If the conference of the States Parties so decides, review conferences may also be held after shorter intervals.

This Article includes the following test on peaceful nuclear explosions (PNEs).

On the basis of a request by any State Party, the Review Conference shall consider the possibility of permitting the conduct of underground nuclear explosions for peaceful purposes. If the Review conference decides by consensus that such nuclear explosions may be permitted, it shall commence work without delay, with a view to recommending to States Parties an appropriate amendment to this Treaty that shall preclude any military benefits of such nuclear explosions.

Article IX - Duration and withdrawal

The treaty is of unlimited duration with withdrawal by any state at six months notice 'if it decides that extraordinary events related to the subject matter of this Treaty have jeopardised its supreme interests'. Notice of such withdrawal shall include a statement of such extraordinary event or events.

France, Russia, the United Kingdom and the United States have each stated that loss of confidence intheir nuclear arsenals would be such an event.

Article X - Status of the Protocol and Annexes

The Annexes to the Treaty and the Protocol and its Annexes 'form an integral part of the Treaty.'

Article XI - Signature

Article XII - Ratification

Article XIII - Accession

CTBT open to all states for signature, is subject to ratification and is open for accession to non-signatory states after entry into force.

Article XIV - Entry into Force

According to the draft text, the CTBT will enter into

force 180 days after the deposit of instruments of ratification of the States listed in Annex 2 (see below).

This Article also allows for a Conference to be held if the Treaty has not entered into force within three years of signature to 'Decide by consensus what measures consistent with international law may be undertaken to accelerate the ratification process'. While such a conference could exert political pressure on states that had not yet ratified, it could not decide to waive any of the entry into force requirements.

The current draft criteria relate to the current operation of nuclear reactors (see notes on Annex 2)., As a specific set of ratifications from states are required for entry into force, any one of them could prevent entry into force.

Article XV - Reservations

'The Articles of and the Annexes to this Treaty shall not be subject to reservations. The provisions of the Protocol to this Treaty and the Annexes to the Protocol shall not be subject to reservations incompatible with the object and purpose of this Treaty.'

Article XVI - Depositary

The United Nations Secretary-General is the Depositary to the Treaty.

Article XVII - Authentic Texts

The Arabic, Chinese, English, French, Russian and Spanish texts are equally authentic.

Annex 1 to the Treaty - List of States Pursuant to Article II, paragraph 28

See Article II, above.

Annex 2 to the Treaty - List of States Pursuant to Article XIV

The criteria for inclusion on the list are that the state should be a member of the CD as at 18 June 1996 and which appear in either Table 1 of the April 1996 edition of 'Nuclear Power Reactors in the World' or Table 1 of the December 1995 edition of 'Nuclear Research Reactors in the World', both published by the International Atomic Energy Agency.

Protocol

The Protocol to the CTBT is divided into three sections; the IMS and IDC functions; on-site inspections; and confidence-building measures. The Protocol also contains two annexes; tables of stations for the various monitoring networks; and a 'List of Characterisation Parameters for International Data Centre Standard Event Screening'.

The International Monitoring System

The IMS is based on four monitoring technologies, specified in the Protocol; seismological, radionuclide, hydroacoustic and infrasound.

Seismological monitoring consists of a network of 50 primary and 120 secondary stations feeding data about vibrations in the Earth to the IDC.

Radionuclide monitoring consists of a network of 80 stations which test the atmosphere for radioactive debris from nuclear explosions. All stations are to be capable of detecting 'relevant particulate matter' with 40 of the stations also able to monitor 'relevant noble gases'; although the noble gas provision has received some opposition.

Hydroacoustic monitoring consists of a network of

11 stations which detects soundwaves travelling through the oceans.

Infrasound monitoring consists of a network of 60 stations which detect soundwaves travelling through the atmosphere at frequencies far below those heard by the human ear.

On-site inspections

The Protocol contains rules for the conduct of on-site inspections. The draft CTBT allows the CTBTO to define the inspection area. However, the inspected State Party has the right 'to make recommendations at any time to the inspection team regarding possible modification of the inspection plan'.

The Protocol allows overflights of the inspection area by the inspection team.

Confidence-building measures

The Protocol allows for voluntary confidence-building measures in the form of notifications by States Parties of large conventional explosions (over 300 tonnes TNT-equivalent) carried out, for example, in mining operations. States Parties may arrange for visits to areas in its territory, in which large quantities of conventional explosives are used, by representatives of the CTBTO or other States Parties.

Stand of Countries

United States of America

In Geneva USA repudiated any threshold for permitted test explosions, thus putting to rest earlier stirrings from the Defence Department about exempting tests below one kiloton. One argument for allowing testing indefinitely was to allow development of mininukes to be used against Third World countries."[26]

Reports appeared about internal dissensions within the US.Administration over the issue of hydro-nuclear testing. A classified paper on options repared by NSC staff member Robert Bell gave four options: Begin Hydronuclear explosions (HNE) now, conduct them after the NPT renewal conference in spring 1995, conduct them after completion of CTBT, or defer a decision indefinitely.

According to a CBO Study, representatives of Department of Defence (DoD) and Joint Chiefs of Staff (JCS) wanted DoE to set aside up to $40 million annually over the next five years to conduct "experiments such as hydronuclear tests" at the Nevada Test site. State Department and DoE officials recommended delaying a decision until after the NPT renewal conference; the Arms Control and Disarmament Agency(ACDA) agreed, and added that such tests were prohibited by US laws but legal experts of other agencies disagreed.[27] Pentagon officials were surprised because they thought when Clinton had suspended nuclear tests in 1993 it was understood that the experiments would be allowed, as they were, during the 1958-61 moratorium.[28]

In August 1994 the ACDA Director, John Holum told the CD plenary that USA sought a CTBT that would bring an end to all nuclear explosions. No thresholds, no exceptions. And by that "I mean not just all explosions, but all tests."[29] USA also proposed (at the CD) "easy out" after five or ten years. This meant that a nation was permitted to withdraw if it felt that five or ten years after the entry into force its supreme national interests were threatened. The State Party would have to give a few months notice and other parties could discuss its implications.[30]

Negotiations at CD ended with a rolling text having three parts. Part 1 contained nine pages of unbracketed text representing present stage of the elaboration of the provisions of draft treaty which commanded a certain degree of consensus. Part 2 having 83 pages of heavily bracketed text contained provisions which needed more extensive negotiations and Part 3 comprised a list of documents containing proposals of delegations.[31]

On 1 December 1994, the UN General Assembly again adopted without a vote a resolution supporting negotiations of a CTB. It called upon CD to proceed to a new phase of negotiation with a renewal of its mandate.[32].

At the end of 1994 during an intersession meeting of the ad hoc committee despite continuing discussions among the P-5, no movement emerged. China still wanted PNE's and Britain and France wanted safety tests. Sweden and Germany continued to seek a ban on preparations. Indonesia wanted to curb simulantions, and several countries wanted the test sites closed.[33]

Coming back to the US position, on 27 January 1994 senior administration officials met to consider the 'easy out' provision and hydronuclear experiment. Defence secretary William Perry and JCS Chairman John Shalikashwili wanted to retain either 'easy-out' solution or provisions permitting higher-yield HNES than the US delegation's proposal of 1.8 kilograms. The meeting failed to resolve the dispute.

In January 1995, USA conveyed to the CD that it had decided to extend the moratorium till September 1996, the time by which it thought the CTB would be concluded and it also withdrew the special "right to withdraw" proposal from the CTBT. The US delegate, however maintained that CTBT must not prohibit activities required to maintain the safety and reliability of "our nuclear stockpile."[34]

In February 1995, Ludwig Dembiniski became the chairman of the ad hoc committee. In February 1995, USA proposed to spend $182 million to maintain the Nevada site in a state of readiness to conduct a test if necessary as part of 1995-96 budget.[35]

By March 1995 there was no change in the position of countries on 'scope'. Britain and France still stayed with exceptional circumstances. China wanted banning any nuclear weapon test which releases energy. Russia still supported a listing of environments. Indonesia wanted the term 'explosives' removed so as to ban inertial confinement fusion, hydrodynamic testings, computer simulations and other activities as well as PNE's.[36]

In April 1995, US Special Representative for Arms Control, Thomas Grant said in an interview that under CTBT "Experiments around 2-4 pounds might be allowed. During the 1958-1961 moratorium we carried these out. This is effectively zero yield. If someone wants us to make a statement to the effect that we are not considering any position other than the zero yield within the US Government, we would be willing to do that."[37]

Disagreements again surfaced at a meeting of the experts of Defence Department and Department of Energy. Participants failed to reach agreement on how such tests could affect the reliability of nuclear weapons. Some Livermore scientists argued that small tests would provide little benefit while costing $10 million. On the other hand, the Los Almos scientists not only wanted to conduct the test but at the higher level.[38]

Secretary for Defence William Perry said in June 1995 at Stanford University that DoD was likely to propose an option falling between no-testing and full-scale testing — either hydronuclear testing or tests of 100 to 200 tons.[39]

The second session of 1995 CD closed on 7 July, with sharp differences over the scope of the treaty. The P-5 could not reach an agreement among themselves; no country had changed its position. The reasons behind the French position to allow tests with yield below 200 tons became clear. Britain and France favoured Pentagon proposal of 500 tons. The G-21 sought to address the question of small tests directly in the language of India (discussed later) and Indonesia tabled a paper banning any testing of nuclear devices. By banning the testing of all devices, this would ban hydronuclear experiments, inertial confinement fusion, hydrodynamic testing and possibly even computer simulation. Most states opposed the Indonesian formulation, saying that a CTBT could only realistically ban the explosions. Some states said that prohibition of activities related to wanted research and production was not appropriate in the CTB negotiations; it could become part of follow-up negotiations. Some states wanted to include the closure of test sites in the 'scope', but others did not want to risk the treaty by overloading it with demands, given the strong opposition by Nuclear-Weapon States.[40]

The earlier consensus among non-nuclear weapon states about turning a blind eye to hydronuclear tests broke down for several reasons including increased awareness about testing at sub- kiloton yields and distrust of nuclear-weapon powers.

Many other issues, including those on verification, international data centre, on-site inspections, the organization and entry into force remained unresolved.

The US Senate voted on 4 August 1995 to spend $ 50 million on hydronuclear tests. It was reported that Jason report submitted to DoE and DoD had concluded that small-scale tests wuld do little to ensure the reliability of the arsenal.[41]

On 11 August 1995, President Bill Clinton said that USA would no longer seek exceptions for low-yield tests. "I am announcing my decision to negotiate a true zero-yield comprehensive test ban that prohibits any nuclear weapon test explosion, or any other nuclear explosion."[42] Clinton also added six `conditions' under which US would agree to a CTBT. The conditions follow the pattern of those of John Kennedy's understanding with the Pantagon to win support for the Partial Test Ban treaty in 1963. The conditions were:

1. "The conduct of a stockpile stewardship programme to ensure a high level of confidence in the safety and reliability of nuclear weapons."
2. "The maintenance of modern nuclear laboratory facilities."
3. "The maintainance of basic capability to ensure nuclear tests" if the US ceases to adhere to the CTBT.
4. Improvement in "treaty monitoring capabilities."
5. Development of intelligence gathering capabilities to "ensure accurate and comprehensive information on worldwide nuclear programmes", and
6. The "understanding" that if the reliability of a weapon type could not be certified, US "would be prepared to withdraw from the CTBT... in order to conduct whatever testing might be required".

Speaking on the General Debate of the 50th General Assembly on 25 September 1995, the US Secretary of State, Warren Christopher talked about "building on the achievement (of the extension of NPT indefnitely). The steps, he outlined, included a CTBT "ready for signature by the time we meet here next year." He said, "The US is committed to a true zero-yield test ban. We urge other nations to join us in that commitment."

CRAFTING A CTBT

Speaking at Plenary session in January 1996, the ACDA Director John Holum (who was reading a message from President Clinton) in response to linkage of CTBT with time-bound framework for complete elimination of nuclear weapons, said, "holding one important goal hostage to another is a same way to fail at both." He also said, "Comprehensive test itself is a profoundly important new constraint especially on the nuclear weapon states... Second, the CTBT is an indispensable step if the ultimate elimination of nuclear weapons is ever to be achieved." [43]

On 26 January 1996, the US Senate in the START II resolution of ratification, held that the country could resume underground nuclear testing if "that is necessary to maintain confidence in the nuclear stockpile". The resolution also noted the need to preserve nuclear weapon competencies. [44]

On 21 April 1996, after Clinton-Yeltsin meet, President Clinton said in a press conference, "We have all agreed to go with the so-called Australian language which is a strict zero-yield comprehensive test ban treaty." [45]

China

In a working paper placed in the CD on 30 March 1994, China tabled its version of the basic structure of the treaty. The noteworthy features (reflecting Chinese concerns) included: activities not prohibited under the treaty; peaceful uses of nuclear energy and peaceful nuclear explosions; non-nuclear explosions and security guarantees of State Parties. [46] On 10 June 1994, China conducted its fortieth explosion. In the announcement made thereafter it said that, China "supports conclusion of CTBT not later than 1996, after negotiations." [47] The arguments were repeated after it conducted the next test. It said, "China will put an end to nuclear tests once the treaty comes into effect." [48]

China advocated peaceful nuclear explosions (PNE's). In Working Group 2 at CD on 9 March 1995, it said that NPT permitted PNE's, arguing that strict examination and monitoring of sites could prevent a clandestine weapon test.[49] Despite supporting the resolution at the 1995 Extension Conference, China on 15 May two days after the conclusion of the Conference, conducted another (42d) test. A statement by Foreign Ministry read: "China strongly calls on the other nuclear-weapon states to respond positively to China's proposal to expeditiously conclude through negotiations, a treaty on `no-first' use of nuclear weapons against each other and reach an agreement on not to use or threaten to use nuclear weapons against non-nuclear-weapon states and nuclear free zones."[50] Japan threatened to cut off aid to China. At the CD on 1 June 1995, China said: "The international community, including China has expressed that the CTBT will be concluded at an early date, but in no case later than 1996. After the treaty has entered into force, China will abide by it and stop testing."[51] In the next CD session, China wanted either a complete zero or a high enough threshold to continue its weapon programme.

At the final part of the 1995 Conference on Disarmament China made its only statement (on 5 September) addressing the criticism of its testing programme. Ambassador Sha Zukang said that China had not held up negotiations and was taking "an active, responsible and constructive part in current negotiations with a view to concluding (the CTBT) not later than 1995."[52]

Speaking at the General Debate in the 50th General Assembly on 27 September 1995, the Chinese Foreign Minister (though made only a passing reference to CTBT) said, "China is supportive of concluding a CTBT no later than 1996 and will continue to work with other

CRAFTING A CTBT   153

countries to this end. Once the treaty enters into force China will stop testing." [53]

In January 1996, China continued to call the proposed ban on PNE unreasonable. However, Wu Xuegian, a vice chair of China Peoples Political Consultative Conference said in a meeting with Japanese legislators that China took "an active stance" on signing the CTBT. [54]

Speaking at the CD Plenary, the Chinese representative Gen. Qian Shaojin said, "All countries are entitled to make their own judgement whether to develop and utilize PNE technology in the light of their own national conditions and economic needs." Qian also questioned the "Zero yield", saying, "it provides no unambiguous definition as to whether or not there would be a nuclear energy release."[55]

On 2 February 1996, the Chinese Ambassador Sha Zukang told CD plenary that a quick completion of a CTBT no later than 1996 had always been the target of the Chinese delegation.[56]

On 6 June 1996, China, in a major policy reversal agreed to drop the demand seeking exception for PNE. Describing it as a technology with "enormous potential", the Chinese representative Sha Zukang said, "China would agree to ban a promising technology just for the sake of banning nuclear weapon test explosions."[57] China, however, added that the ban was "temporary... namely China would agree to a provision that the possibility of permitting the conduct of PNE's should be considered by a review conference of State Parties". As another gesture it dropped its demand for a separate article on negative security assurances to non-nuclear powers and a mutual 'no-first' use of nuclear weapons among nuclear-weapon states (although he did call for "due attention" to be given to these issues). China held that entry into force should be subject to the condition that all the states technologically capable of conducting nuclear explosions would join. It also agreed that some language on nuclear disarmament be included in the language of the treaty. Softening its stand on opposition to NTM, Sha Zukang said, "If NTM data were to be used as a part of the basis for requesting OSI, they must be technical, reliable, verifiable and obtained in consistence with international law".

China conducted another test on 8 June, at Lop Nor, after which it announced that it would conduct one more test before Septmber and then observe a moratorium. While welcoming the moratorium a number of countries expressed concern and disappointment (on 13 June 1996). In their statement at the CD they said that the test was not called for at a time when great efforts were being made to conclude negotiations on CTBT within two weeks. These countries included Canada, New Zealand, Switzerland, Germany, Australia, Mexico, Japan, Chile, the Republic of Korea, Norway , Sweden, Belgium and Mongolia.

The Ambassador of China to the Conference said in response that it had not been easy for China to take a decision on imposition of a moratorium, as it had so far conducted fewest number of tests among the declared nuclear powers. He added that certain nuclear superpowers had made some unwarranted remarks about these tests which had been carried out based on legitimate security concerns. China called upon these countries to focus instead on negotiations in order to ensure their successful conclusion.[58] China, on 18 June 1996, rejected the Japanese demand to cancel further nuclear tests.

France

France under President Mitterand did not conduct any nuclear test. He believed that his successor would not resume testing for fear of offending the whole world by relaunching nuclear overarming.[59] In late May 1994, the French Government dropped plans for parliamentary vote on the resumption of tests. Defence Minister Leotand said that the decision on testing should rest with the executive branch not the legislature.[60]

The French policy on CTBT was described by Prime Minister Balladur in a speech to the Institute of Advanced Studies of National Defence in Paris: "In no way was it about envisaging the elimination of nuclear weapons, or of seeking to undermine the position of the nuclear power." Any drift to this effect would meet with France's opposition. He also said that the treaty could only come into force after its ratification by the nuclear powers alone, or by a number of countries *not including* the threshold countries (emphasis added).[61]

Reports of French plans to spend $1.7 billion under the new defence budget on simulated nuclear testing, appeared in mid-June 1994. Earlier the Rapporteur of the new military programming law, Arthur Paecht said on 10 May 1994 that according to unanimous recommendation of all experts consulted, the resumption of nuclear tests was indispensable. As to the PALEN (Preparation of Linetation of Nuclear Testing) test simulation programme it "would not suffice to ensure the development of new nuclear changes."[62]

Amidst reports of four of the five nuclear powers wanting to continue nuclear testing, were some stating that the French wanted consideration of as much as 100 tons.[63] According to another report, France wanted to make it clear that it could result in unintentional yield of up to 10 tons.[64] A report in March 1995 said that France wanted a limit of 100-200 tons for a tiny blast.[65]

On 13 June 1995, the new President Jacques Chirac informing a news conference that France would resume testing in September said: "I made this decision because

I considered it necessary in the higher interest of our nation... The decision is, of course, irrevocable." He added that France would conduct eight tests between September 1995 and May 1996, halt all tests by May 1996 and sign the CTBT. "In order to do that, it had to be in a position to guarantee the security and reliability of its deterrent force and it also had to be able to switch to simulation like other countries."[66]

A panel of senior military experts consulted by Chirac recommended in an update to the panel's report issued eighteen months earlier that France should continue the series of tests interrupted in 1992 when another four were scheduled and do up to 20 tests altogether. The panel concluded that to finish the tests by autumn of 1996, the expected time of signing of the CTBT, the testing would have to begin by October 1995.[67]

Insisting that the tests would not harm the environment, Chirac said that Mitterand's decision to halt testing was premature because France had not completed the development of simulation techniques.

Prime Minister Alan Juppe said that the new tests had only two aims: "To verify the safety of weapons currently available and to pass on to the level of simulation."

French defence experts disclosed the opinion of the military leadership that up to a dozen tests were necessary to verify the effectiveness of warhead stocks, in order to ensure the viability of the new warhead for the M-5 SLBM, to enhance computer simultation plans, and to experiment with the miniature warheads.[68]

Defence Minister Charles Milton, however, said that the testing was under way to design new weapons, to develop theatre weapons intended for use on a beattlefield, or to miniaturize them. "Our nuclear arsenal remains one of deterrence."[69]

CRAFTING A CTBT

International reactions to the French decision on testing were varied. USA regretted the decision but it was grateful that France had pledged to join the CTBT and had supported the NPT. The Chinese hoped that "France will work with other countries towards efforts to reach CTBT no later than 1996." The North Koreans called France "deceptive". The Russian Foreign Minister Andrei Kozyrev recalled (at the CD) the NPT decision calling for maximum restraint. He said, "We find it hard to agree with those who allege that the continuation or resumption of nuclear tests is not in that provision."[70]

The 15-Nation South Pacific Forum issued a statement on 14 June 1995 condemning the decision and noting France's signature on NPT decision.[71]

Reactions of New Zealand and Australia were stronger. Australia froze defence links, banning any ships or planes involved in transporting goods to Murora. It also eliminated Dassault from contention for a $360 million contract for fighters for the Royal Australian Air Force. New Zealand Prime Minister Jim Bolger told Parliament that the government would halt military ties with France.

At the CD session also delegates focussed on French testing. Japan said that France had "betrayed the confidence of non-nuclear weapon states." Norway feared that the decision would complicate efforts to prevent nuclear non-proliferation and South Africa called on states to honour both the letter and spirit of NPT decision. Iran, Myanmar and Mexico also criticized the French decision.[72]

The French delegate at the CD said that when France opposed Mexican proposal to include a commitment to maintain the testing moratorium in the NPT 'Principles and Objectives', agreeing to "utmost restraint" instead, it was "well known and understood" that France was keeping the option open for resuming nuclear tests.

Other delegates described the NTB talks as "lacking incentive" and demoralizing.

Reports of New Zealand and Australia planning to bring France before the International Court of Justice appeared when Australian Prime Minister Paul Keating met New Zealand's Jim Bolger in Melbourne on 22 July 1995.[73]

France nevertheless made no changes in its decision on testing. President Chirac rejected the Socialist call for referendum on testing. J. Bouchard, Director of CEA said that one test would be the last in the series to qualify a TN 75 warhead; secondly, weapon developers wanted to make necessary modifications in its weapons already tested to prevent these from becoming obsolete. Thirdly, the tests would allow designers to acquire necessary physical reference points for simulations.[74]

Subsequently on 1 August 1995, the French government withdrew its ambassador from Australia and also announced an accelerated time-table for testing saying that four devices were ready.[75]

In the CD, the French delegate maintained that France would support a truly comprehensive test ban and that it endorsed the language of the Australian proposal.[76]

On 8 August 1995, New Zealand went before the International Court of Justice seeking its intervention to order France to stop the tests. New Zealand based its case on a ruling by the ICJ in 1974 that ordered France to stop the tests. France refused to recognize the Court's jursidiction in that case. In the present case, New Zealand pressed its arguments before the ICJ on 11 September 1995.[77]

Speaking during the General Debate of the 50th UN General Assembly the French Foreign Minister Herve de Charette said that the testing programme had been "temporarily suspended". He said that the test "now under way has no other purpose than to enable us to sign the treaty banning nuclear tests immediately." Refuting strongly that France would reconsider its decision on acceding to CTBT he said, "once again I repeat this is final test series, limited to what is strictly necessary and held under conditions that have proved to be harmless. It will enable us to adhere as early as possible to the future treaty banning tests indefinitely". Calling the CTBT as the "most important" goal, he said CTBT negotiations should "ensure the ban is total." [78]

On 29 January 1996, Jacques Chirac announced "the definitive end to France's nuclear test," adding that "thanks to this last series of tests which have just finished, France will have an efficient and modern defence system which will last." [79] The next day the French Defence Minister said, "The six explosion made it possible to accumulate data to an extent rarely done before."[80]

Russia

The Russians support a test ban. Ostensibly, Russia does not need nuclear warheads to deal with the West. Besides, what was previously the major Soviet site is now in independent Kazakhstan. In November 1994, some Russian nuclear scientists called for resumption of nuclear testing. Radi Ilkayev, a leading expert at the Federal Nuclear Center said, "Nuclear tests are necessary for preserving the safety and reliability of nuclear weapons. Experts in nuclear weapons can only preserve their skills by carrying out real tests."[81] Many Russain experts claimed that lack of testing since 1990 had left Russia far behind because it had performed fewer tests than the United States.

The Secretary of Russian Security Council, Valeriy Manilov said on 9 April 1995, "We are faced with a very serious problem of verification and development of actually assured, most effective mechanisms of ensuring in particular, the safety of munitions that have already become obsolete. Doing so without conducting tests would be problematic... There is a chance that upon reflection, we would estimate a number of tests which would rule out the possibility of a potentially gross violation of nuclear security." [82]

In 1995 April reports of Kazakhastan destroying its nuclear charge at Semipalatinsk appeared. Earlier report had talked about a Russian-Kazakhastan group implementing a project to that effect. Russia was to cover the cost, in excess of one billion roubles.[83] In June 1995, at the CD, Russia criticized France for testing saying the extreme restraint on this particular issue should mean the same for all. In the course of the deliberations in August 1995 Russia remained worried about Chinese advances in missile and warhead technology. Some believed that its advocacy of a 10 ton limit disguised a desire to conduct 100 ton decoupled tests which would appear as 10 ton tests. Some held that Yeltsin would support 'zero-yield' if directly asked by Clinton, though the military might want concessions in return, such as the revival of Peaceful Nuclear Explosions(PNE's).[84]

Speaking on 27 September 1995 at the 50th General Assembly's General Debate, the Russian Foreign Minister Andrei Kozyrev of Russia said that the extension of NPT was "necessary as a matter of priority" to conclude the CTBT as early as possible "but not later than 1996". In the meantime he called for "a universal and permanent moratorium on nuclear tests." [85]

Speaking on 7 March 1996, the Russian delegate said that the treaty "should not contain any thresholds", but did not use the terms 'zero yield'. He opposed Indian proposal for linkage between CTB and time-bound elimination of nuclear weapons, saying it would "only hamper the treaty".[86]

Two specialists from the Azamas — 16 nuclear research centre — were quoted on 26 March 1996,as saying that Russia would not sign CTBT if NATO expanded eastward.[87]

On 20 April 1996 President Boris Yeltsin of Russia and the leaders of the G-7 called for a speedy comprehensive test ban.[88] On 21 April 1996, at a press conference following a Clinton-Yeltsin meeting, Yeltsin said, "Not all nuclear states participated in yesterday's meeting of the eight. Now, with the others, we are going to have to do a little work, especially with China."[89]

United Kingdom

Britain's position on CTBT was contained in its Defence White Paper 1994. It said:

"Committing ourselves to negotiate a CTB has not been an entirely easy decision for us. We have until now relied on a minimal programme of underground nuclear testing, complemented by a range of above ground experimental work and computer simulation, as a cost-effective means of ensuring our ability to underwrite the safety and reliability of our nuclear warheads. With the possibility of concluding a CTBT, our plans are now based on use and further development of simulation and alternative technologies so as to provide a basis for the continued underwriting of warhead safety and reliability in a situation where it is no longer possible to conduct a nuclear test."[90]

To a question in the Parliament in June 1994, the Minister of State for Defence procurement replied: "Previously, a minimal programme of nuclear testing has been an important part of preserving the safety and reliability of our weapons. We now aim to use and develop alternative technologies."[91]

On 21 June 1994, the Minister of State for Foreign and Commonwealth office, Baroness Chalten said in the House of Lords, "We never made a demand that safety tests should be excluded from the treaty."[92]

On 18 January 1995, Foreign Secretary Douglas Hurd told Parliament's Foreign Affairs Committee that Britain viewed the CTBT as a non-proliferation rather than a nuclear disarmament measure.[93]

On 6 April 1995, Britain announced that it would drop "exceptional explosions" as part of 'Scope'. He added: "This in no way diminishes our responsibility to ensure the safety and reliability of our nuclear weapons. I would like to state for the record that we consider that the `Scope' Article should not be interpreted as prohibiting the UK in common with other nuclear weapons states, from fulfilling its responsibilities to maintain the safety and reliability of its nuclear weapons."[94]

The junior defence minister Lord Henby told the House of Lords on 20 June 1995 that the British government would not rule out resumption of testings. But he assured peers: "we have no plans to test while the US moratorium is in force."[95]

The British government refused to criticize France either for resumption of testing or for ramming of the Rainbow Warrior II. The Minister of State in the Foreign Office, David Davis told the House of Commons: "First and foremost, President Chirac made it clear that France's national security needs could not be met in any other way. I do not believe that it is for us to seek to second-guess his judgement on this... The French decision and their reiterated commitment to a CTBT are a constructive contribution towards achieving that goal."[96]

Notes and References

1. CD/12.12.
2. CD/12131 (Mexico), CD/1232 (Sweden), CD/1235 and Corr. (Australia).
3. CD/1273/Rev.1.
4. See Rebecca Johnson & Sean Howard, *A Comprehensive Test Ban: Disappointing Progress*, ACRONYM No.3, September 1994, for a summary of negotiations in 1994.
5. *Arms Control Reporter*, 1996, p. 608, B 398.
6. *Arms Control Reporter*, 1996, p. 608, B 410.
7. Rebecca Johnson, *Geneva Update*, No.28, June 1,1996.
8. See Rebecca Johnson, *Indefinite Extension of the Non-proliferation Treaty: Risks and Reckonings*, ACRONYM No.7, September 1995, for the full text of the NPT decisions and the discussions of their implications.
9. Cited in *Basic Papers*, May 30,1996, p.1
10. CD/NTB/WP.222.
11. FBIS-Near East and South Asia, January 31,1996 citing *The Nation*, January 29,1996.
12. *Arms Control Reporter*, 1996, p. 608, B 389.
13. Ibid, p. 608 B 395.
14. *Arms Control Reporter*,1996, p.607, B.396.
15. British American Security Information Council (BASIC) Papers, May 30,1996, p.3.
16. DPI Release, DC/96/26, June 6,1996
17. Rebecca Johnson, *Geneva Update* No. 28,June 1,1996.
18. *Arms Control Reporter*, 1996, p.608, B 383.
19. *FBIS-SOV*, January 24,1996.
20. *Arms Control Reporter*, 1996, p.608, B 396.
21. *New York Times*, March 8,1996.
22. CD/1385, February 26,1996.
23. *DPI Release*, DC/96/26, June 6,1996.
24. *International Herald Tribune*, February 1,1996.
25. British American Security Information Council(BASIC) Papers, May 30,1996, p.3

26. Paul C. Warnke, 'Strategic Nuclear Policy and Non-Proliferation', *Arms Control Today*, Vol. 24, No.4, May 1994, p.4.
27. *Washington Post*, July 22,1994 and Ibid. July 28,1994.
28. *Arms Control Reporter*, 1995, p.608, B 313.
29. ACDA, Press Release, August 4,1994.
30. CD/1273/Rev.1, September 5,1994.
31. *Arms Control Reporter*, 1995, p.608, B 326.
32. A/Res./49 January 9,1995.
33. *Nuclear Proliferation News*, December 20,1994.
34. CD/PV/693, 31 January,1995.
35. *Arms Control Reporter*, 1995, p.608, B 323.
36. *Nuclear Proliferation News*, 21st March,1995.
37. Interview to Dan Plebsch and Stephen Young in *Basic Reports*, April 14,1995.
38. *Washington Post*, 18 June,1995.
39. Ibid, 23 June,1995.
40. *Arms Control Reporter*, 1995. p.608, B 350.
41. *New York Times*, August 12,1995.
42. *Disarmament Times*, Vol. XVIII, No.5, September 10,1995, p.1.
43. *Arms Control Reporter*, 1996, p.608, B 285.
44. Ibid. p.608, B 298.
45. Ibid. p.608 B 414.
46. CD/NTB/WP 51, *Nuclear Non-Proliferation News*, May 27,1994.
47. FBIS - China, May 2,1994, quoting Beijing Radio April 29,1994.
48. FBIS - China, 7 October 1994 citing Xinhua 7 October 1994.
49. Rebecca Johnson's report in ACRONYM Booklet No.6, April 1995.
50. ACR 602B-330: *Washington Post*, May 23,1995.
51. *Nuclear Proliferation News*, June 1,1995.
52. Rebecca Johnson, 'Some Progress on Test Ban Talks', *Disarmament Times*, Vol. XVIII, No.5, p.1, 19 September,1995.
53. *Disarmament Times*, Vol. XVIII, No.5, October 11,1995, p. 4.
54. *Washington Times*, January 12,1996.

CRAFTING A CTBT

55. *Disarmament Diplomacy*, January 1996, cited in *Arms Control Reporter*, 1996, 608, B 389.
56. *People's Daily*, February 10,1996.
57. DPI Release DC/96/26, June 6,1996.
58. DPI, Release, DC/96/27, June 13, 1996.
59. *Nuclear Non-Proliferation News*, 13 May 1994.
60. Ibid 10 June 1994.
61. FBIS - West Europe, 15 August 1994, citing *Logos* May 10,1994.
62. FBIS - West Europe, May 16,1994.
63. *Nuclear Non-Proliferation News*, 24 June,1994.
64. *Washington Post*, 22 July 1994.
65. Thomas Cochran and Christopher Paine in NRDC Nuclear Weapons Databook, 'The Role of Hydronuclear Tests and other Low-yield Nuclear Explosions and their Status under a Comprehensive Test Ban'; released on 27 March 1994,cited in *Arms Control Reporter*, 1995, p.608 B, 327.
66. FBIS-West Europe, 14 June 1995, citing France-2 Television, 13 June 1995 (live).
67. *Jane's Defense Weekly*, June 17,1995, also see *USA Today*, June 7,1995.
68. FBIS - West Europe, 15 June,1995.
69. FBIS - West Europe, June 20,1995.
70. *Washington Post*, 14 June 1995, UN Mission (N. Korea) Press Release (22 June 1995), *New York Times*, June 30, 1995.
71. South Pacific Forum Statement. A/50/224 (20th June 1995); FBIS-West Europe, 20 June 1995; *Christian Science Monitor*, 12 July 1995.
72. *Nuclear Non-Proliferation News*, June 30,1995.
73. FBIS-East Asia, 25 July 1995.
74. FBIS - West Europe, 28 July 1995.
75. *Washington Times*, August 3,1995, Also see ibid, August 10,1995.
76. *Arms Control Reporter*, 1995.
77. *Disarmament Times*, Vol. XVIII, No.5, September 19,1995, p.1. 78. *Disarmament Times*, Vol XVIII, No.6, 11 October 1995, p.4.

79. *International Herald Tribune*, January 30,1996, p.1.
80. *Washington Post*, February 2,1996.
81. *Arms Control Reporter*, 1995, p.608, B 314, citing AP report (November 3,1994).
82. FBIS - SOV, April 19,1995 citing Vladimir Ostov in *Moskovskiye Novosti*, April 6-23, 1995.
83. FBIS- SOV, April 13,1994.
84. *Arms Control Reporter*, 1995, p. 608 B 357.
85. *Disarmament Times*, Vol XVIII No.6, 11 October 1995, p. 4.
86. *New York Times*, March 8,1996.
87. *Arms Control Reporter*, 1996, 608 B 408.
88. *New York Times*, April 21, 1996.
89. *Arms Control Reporter*, 1996, 608, B 414, citing White House Transcript.
90. *Trust and Verify*, November 1994.
91. *Arms Control Reporter*, 1995, 608, B.309.
92. Ibid, p.310.
93. Basic Notes, March 1995. p.1.
94. *Nuclear Proliferation News*, April 25,1995.
95. *Arms Control Reporter*, 1995, p.608, B.345.
96. *Arms Control Reporter*, 1995, p.608, B.346.

Chapter 6
India's Response

Developments upto 1993

India categorically proposed suspension of nuclear-weapon tests for the first time on 2 April 1954. It at all started from the Parliamentary debates in India, in which the attention of the Indian Government was drawn to matters of urgent public importance created by the explosion of hydrogen bomb by the United States of America on 1 March 1953. The test was part of the series of atmospheric tests called 'Operation Castle'. It produced a yield of 15 megaton (over twice of the expected yield) and dramatically highlighted the damages of radioactive fall-out. The fall-out killed Japanese fishermen.

In a statement made on 2 April 1954, Prime Minister Jawaharlal Nehru urged for "some sort of, what may be called `Standstill Agreement' in respect, at least, of these actual explosions, even if arrangements about the discontinuance of explosions, even if arrangements about the discontinuance of production and stockpiling, must await more substantial agreements amongst those principally concerned."[1]

The other aspects of this proposal included:

1. Full publicity by those principally concerned in the

production of these weapons, and by the United Nations, of the extent of the destructive power and the known effects of these weapons and also adequate indication of the extent of the unknown but probable effects.

2. Immediate (and continuing) private meetings of the sub-committee of the Disarmament Commission to consider the 'Standstill' proposal, pending decisions of prohibitions and controls, etc., to which the Disarmament Commission is asked by the General Assembly to address itself.

3. Active steps by states and peoples of the world, who though not directly concerned with the production of these weapons, are very much concerned by possible use of them, and also at present, with these experiments and their effects.

Later a letter was delivered by India to the Secretary-General of the United Nations transmitting extracts from the statement made by the Prime Minister of India in the House of the People (Lok Sabha) on the subject of the hydrogen bombs.[2] It envisaged suspension of nuclear-weapon tests. This letter was referred to the Disarmament Commission for its consideration. But the Indian proposal did not receive enthusiastic treatement. Nevertheless, as a gesture of goodwill, on the request of the Indian representative to the chairman of the Disarmament Commission, Indian letter was annexed to the fourth report of the Disarmament Commission,[3] and the Indian proposal was referred to the sub-Committee of the Disarmament Commission.

In an 'Explanatory Memorandum' sent to the Secretary-General on 'Dissemination of information on the effects of atomic radiation and the effects of experimental explosions of thermo-nuclear bombs' proposed for inclusion in the agenda of the tenth regular session of the General Assembly, it was *inter alia*, stated:

"The way in which radioactive material produced in the tests of nuclear and thermonuclear weapons is dissipated over the world is not yet fully known. There is a marked difference of opinion among scientists as to the long-term consequences of detonating nuclear and thermonuclear bombs for experimental purposes more particularly with regard to genetic effects while almost all are agreed that ultimately the background radiation could increase to a level which would endanger the existence of mankind. Many consider that a stage has already been reached when further experimental explosion of atomic weapons may have disastrous results for the entire human species some hundred years hence.

"Since all nations of the world and not merely the nations conducting the experiment, may suffer as a result of the after effects of tests of nuclear and thermonuclear bombs and other activities undertaken by various countries for development of atomic energy, the Government of India considers it is essential to set up immediately an international organization which will collect and coordinate the data on immediate and long-term consequences of nuclear radiation as well as the known effects of experimental explosions of the hydrogen and nuclear bombs and inform the world of the same." [4]

Even after the early setbacks, India continued to make requests for the cessation of nuclear-weapon tests.[5] Indian resolution referred to the Disarmament Commission emphasized the study of ways and means of establishing an "armament truce" pending agreement on disarmament convention.[6] The Soviet Union endorsed Indian proposal and in turn proposed discontinuance of atomic and hydrogen tests as first-stage measures to be carried out in 1956.[6a]

In a broadcast message in January 1956, Prime Minister Jawaharlal Nehru said:

"If these terrible weapons (atomic bomb and hydrogen bomb) are let loose on humanity, all our hopes are dashed to pieces and humanity perishes. We have protested against production and experimentation of these weapons. If these experiments of explosion of hydrogen bomb go on, eminent scientists tell us that the future of humanity is imperilled. And yet we have recently had such an experiment in the Soviet Union and we are told that there is going to be another in Pactific areas. All that is of tremendous practical importance to every human being and it raises moral issues of great significance.

"We have put forward Panchsheela and spoken of peaceful co-existences. All these has no meaning if hydrogen bomb pursues its triumphant and malevolent character."[7]

* * * * *

"We could make a beginning even now if the great powers would agree to cessation of explosions of weapons of mass distruction by stopping further manufacture of these weapons and also by making at least a token beginning in abandoning thermonuclear weapons by publicly dismantling at least a few of them."[7a]

The Indian representative presented a *note verbale* to the Disarmament Commission subsequently at the invitation of the Chairman of Disarmament Commission. Indian representative also took a seat at the negotiating table. He built his case for the cessation of nuclear tests for destructive purposes on moral, humanitarian and health grounds. Further, he felt that the suspension of these tests would be first step in nuclear disarmament and check the spread of nuclear weapons.[8]

On the question of secret nuclear tests, he believed that no "concealment of any effective character is possible in regard to explosions." No nation, he added, had the right to contaminate the earth, the air and the seas of the world. He said that the agreement should be observed on the basis of solemn obligations such as international treaties, and the problem of control should not come in the way of meeting of minds.[9]

The Indian suggestions made little impact on the members. Except Yugoslavia and the Soviet Union, the member countries did not agree on the proposed suspension of nuclear-tests explosions. The Indian proposal did not envisage any sort of guarantee to implement the proposal. The proposal was not acceptable to the West.

In 1957 India (and Sweden) suggested a moratorium on nuclear-weapon tests.[10] Later in the year, realizing the importance of inspection and control, India suggested a system "which should be carried out by a body of people who would be selected in equal numbers from those holding different points of view, who should then invite other countries which are not nearly so committed on this matter, so that the whole problem could be looked at technically in that way."[11] Later India made a proposal for the cessation of nuclear and thermonuclear weapon tests with the same proposal of inspection and control.[12] Iceland, Poland, Romania and the Soviet Union supported the Indian resolution but it was rejected.[13]

Prime Minister Nehru then made an appeal to both the Superpowers to stop all nuclear test explosions and bring about effective disarmament.[14] The then Chairman of Soviet Council of Ministers, Bulganin, agreed to his suggestion.[15] The then President of the United States, Eisenhower, however reiterated the proposal made by him earlier in which suspension of nuclear tests was wedded to the progress toward cut-off.[16]

India also co-sponosred a resolution urging France to refrain from conducting nuclear tests in Sahara.[17]

India took the initiative in the 14th General Assembly session proposing the question of suspension of nuclear and thermonuclear tests to be put on the agenda.[18] Subsequently it submitted a 24-powered draft resolution asking the states concerned, in general, to continue their voluntary suspension of tests, and other states to desist from such tests.[19] The then Indian representative reminded that India had brought the question before the General Assembly every year since 1954 and that a cessation of nuclear weapon test explosions would constitute the first major breakthrough.[20] In 1960, India repeated its performance by bringing the issue to the UN General Assembly. Although India wished that the issue be discussed separately, it was considered along with other related problems of disarmament.[21]

India co-sponsored two draft resolutions on the question of suspension of nuclear tests. The Indian representative, maintained that the treaty should provide for total suspension of tests, including the underground ones. He said that India did not subscribe to the view that underground explosions should be allowed to the members of the "nuclear club"[22] In the next session (sixteenth), India made an appeal to great powers requesting them not to resume testing.[23]

When negotiations on nuclear test-ban treaty were resumed after a long gap, the Indian Defence Minister said at the Eighteen-Nation Disarmament Committee (ENDC) that the issue was of high priority and asked the great powers not to conduct nuclear tests while the Geneva Conference was sitting.[24] As a matter of fact, this suggestion was made by the then Prime Minister of India in his reply to the Lok Sabha debate on the President's Address.[25]

India became a member of the drafting committee of what eventually constituted the eight-power 'compromise' referendum of 16 April 1962, seeking ban on nuclear tests, which did not go very far, despite repeated pleas.[26] At home Nehru continued to describe them (nuclear tests) as "crime against humanity." [27]

On Partial Test Ban, India held that it would be valuable "but it is not the solution". The Indian representative to ENDC, Arthur Lall, asked the nuclear powers to come to a conclusion (on nuclear test ban) "taking into account constructive recommendations of their own high-level scientists in the field."[28]

On Indian request, the UN General Assembly included an agenda item on 25 June 1962, for "the urgent need for suspsension of nuclear and thermonuclear tests."[29] The Indian representative emphasized the importance of the eight-nation memorandum according to which it was the international commission and not parties to the treaty which would decide whether further clarification was necessary in order to determine its nature. The memorandum had also stated that if a party had not cooperated fully to establish the nature of the event, the other parties should be free to act as they deemed fit.[30]

In an explanatory memorandum submitted subsequently on 9 July 1962, the Indian representative, C.S. Jha, added:

"Nuclear powers continue to engage in testing, which is causing grave concern not only because of the radiation hazards to which present and future generations are being subjected but also because it is leading to an intensification of arms race itself. The succession of nuclear tests by great powers with an avowed intention of technological perfection of weapons of mass destruction has an aggravating effect on international situation.

"The Government of India remains convinced that it is more imperative than ever that all nuclear and thermonuclear tests should cease forthwith and remain suspended pending urgent conclusion of necessary agreements in this regard."[31]

In November 1962, the Indian representative said in ENDC that a small quota of invitations for on-site inspections should be fixed. He added that the quota could only be fixed in the first instance for the first year because instruments might improve and other factors might arise which would justify a revision of the stated quota of invitations.[32]

Shortly after President Kennedy's announcement of the commencement of negotiations in July 1963, India once again requested for inculsion in the agenda of the eighteenth session of the UN General Assembly the item on the "urgent need for suspension of all nuclear and thermonuclear tests".[33] Subsequently the proposed item was considered by the First Committee in October 1963.

In a letter dated 10 October 1964 to the Secretary-General, the then Indian permanent representative to the UN, B.N. Chakravarty, said that the treaty (PTBT) was an important landmark in the disarmament discussions. It restricted the development of nuclear weapons and implied renunciation of the manufacture of these weapons of mass destruction on part of those non-nuclear states which subscribed to the test-ban treaty. But as the treaty did not specifically prohibit manufacture, acquisition, receipt or transference of these weapons, the conclusion of an agreement on non-proliferation of nuclear weapons would be the next logical step after the signing of the test-ban treaty.[34]

In a statement in the Lok Sabha, the Foreign Minister Swaran Singh said on 10 May 1966, that the Government of India condemned the action taken by the Chinese

Government which, "constitutes, a threat to world peace, a grave hazard to the health and safety of people living in areas of the world likely to be affected by the radioactive fall-out resulting from this explosion and generally contrary to the interests of the humanity at large. He added that India had made a careful assessment of the situation after the first nuclear device was exploded by China, in consultation with Defence services chiefs and atomic energy experts. Therefore the mere fact that China had carried out its third nuclear explosion did not vitiate its earlier conclusion, though at the same time the policy was kept under constant review.[35]

Refuting Pakistan's allegations of Indian plans to conduct a nuclear test, the Indian representative said in August 1966 that India "has consistently advocated its extension to cover underground tests. It is a matter of greatest regret to India that the agreement has not been reached on total prohibition of nuclear weapon tests."[36]

As the NPT debate picked up, India vociferously opposed moves by the nuclear-weapon powers to deny peaceful nuclear explosions by non-nuclear weapon powers. Thus in a statement made in the First Committee in 1968 the Indian representative, Azim Hussain said.

"There should, therefore, in the first instance, be a total prohibition of all nuclear explosion for all states, nuclear as well as non-nuclear. Thereafter the conduct of explosions considered necessary for peaceful purposes should be dealt with as exceptions and should be under international supervision and with safeguards equally applicable to all. For that purpose an international regime would have to be established for all states."[37]

Reiterating this and further elaborating, the Indian representative said in May 1969:

"A separate international agreement needs to be

negotiated for regulating the conduct of nuclear explosions for peaceful purposes. Such an international agreement would have to legislate the purposes for which explosions would be permitted... Various matters (health etc) would require a whole complex of rules and regulations laying down and governing an international regime of nuclear explosion for peaceful purposes. It is then clear that for establishment of such a regime, a separate, self-contained and comprehensive international agreement would be indespensable."

India also emphatically said that there should be no piecemeal modification of the PTBT to provide for PNE's. Such modifications as were necessary should be conceived as integral part of a comprehensive international agreement on peaceful explosions, "because on no account are we willing to accept a position under which nuclear explosion for peaceful purposes would in years to come become the monopoly of nuclear-weapon powers alone." [38]

The same stand was reiterated in the General Assembly in December that year and in the First Committee in November 1970.

Intervening in a Lok Sabha debate in April 1970 the then Prime Minister, Mrs. Indira Gandhi said:

"The main question he (Samar Guha) has asked is why we are preventing the Atomic Energy Commission from going in for nuclear blasting and for using nuclear energy for engineering: why we are opposed to it ? Now, Sir, we are not at all opposed to the use of nuclear energy for peaceful purpose when a meaningful application of more economic significance is identified. This was an important part in our opposition to the Nuclear Non-Proliferation Treaty — the NPT bans not only nuclear weapons but also other nuclear devices and therefore, one has to keep this in view." [39]

Reaffirming the plea in 1970 the Indian representative said that the IAEA should take the responsibility (of an international service for PNE's) and provide these services on non-discriminatory basis upon request by member states.[40] This was reiterated in October 1972 in the First Committee of the UN General Assembly.

On 15 November 1972, in a written answer, the Prime Minister Mrs. Indira Gandhi said in the Lok Sabha that the Atomic Energy Commission was constantly reviewing the technology of underground nuclear explosions both from the theoretical and experimental angles and (was) also taking into account their potential economic benefits and possible environmental hazards.[41]

Almost repeating this statement Mrs. Gandhi stated in Rajya Sabha on 15 November 1973. "It is only after satisfactory answer to all these problems (environmental and ecological) are available that the question of actual underground tests for peaceful purposes can be considered."[41a]

The Government of India announced on 18 May 1974 that it had carried out a peaceful nuclear explosion experiment using an impolosion device. The explosion was carried out at a depth of more than 100 metres.

As part of the programme of study of peaceful nuclear explosions, the Government of India had undertaken a programme to keep itself abreast of developments in this technology particularly with reference to its use in the field of mining and earth-moving operations. The Atomic Energy Commission, Government of India, also stated that India had no intention of producing nuclear weapons and reiterated its strong opposition to military uses of nuclear explosions.[42]

The Indian representative, Samarendra Kundu said in May 1978 that a CTB treaty should be properly seen not as an end in itself but as a means to achieve the ultimate objective of a world free from nuclear weapons. A CTB treaty "should be followed or preferably accompanied by other measures, such as cessation of fissile material for weapon purpose etc... Furthermore, we are convinced that a CTB treaty without the participation of France and China, while welcome as a first step, would not be truly effective."[43] He also said, "we have not and we do not intend to carry out any nuclear weapon tests."[44]

In 1979, Gharekhan, the Indian representative, said that as evidence of "goodwill and political will" to bring about a test ban, the nuclear-weapon states should observe "moratorium" on nuclear testing pending the conclusion of a comprehensive test ban agreement. India welcomed the report submitted by seismic experts contained in the Document CD/43. (For a long time India was the only developing country to take part in Ad Hoc Group of Experts). It expressed a hope that the cost of data centres would be borne by host countries. Stating that the recommendation would have some financial implications for countries participating in the effort, Gharekhan said that India would consider the recommendation about the standardized equipment.[45]

While stating that the mandate of Experts group should continue, he wondered if states which were negotiating would have the necessary ability to verify compliance through national technical means.

In 1980 again, India appealed to the world community in CD to see the treaty as part of complete disarmament, which should be negotiated multilaterally, and to treat the problem not merely as technical (read verification) but also political agreement between nuclear-weapon states on a moratorium on nuclear-weapon tests.[46]

In the discussion in CD, the Indian representative discussed the report of Secretary-General to the General Assembly on the issue, saying that "intensive negotiations" sought in the Secretary-General's report could only take place in a multilateral forum where all nuclear-weapon states were present—ad hoc working group being the best machinery.

Interestingly, India said that the choice was to "conclude an adequately verifiable comprehensive test ban treaty now, and thereby contribute to the reverssal of nuclear arms race or we decline to accept the comprehensive test-ban treaty with the levels of verification that are already available to us."[47]

India also made a plea that while the trilateral talks could continue, the nuclear-weapon powers should agree to participate in negotiations to be conducted in an ad hoc working group. India also sought 'moratorium' on testing and assosciation of CD in negotiations.[48]

Speaking at the special session of the UN General Assembly in June 1978, the then prime Minister, Morarji Desai, said that substantial reduction within a prescribed time-schedule in the weapons and forces of violence must consist of, *inter alia,* a comprehensive test ban treaty with provision for safeguards to prevent a breach of the treaty, which in his view could only be through independent inspection.[49]

In a message to the UN Conference on Disarmament Mrs. Gandhi elaborated on a programme of action to bring about total disarmament. It included, *inter alia,* immediate suspension of all nuclear weapons tests.[50]

Speaking in July 1980, the Indian representative A.P. Venkateswaran said in the CD that there was an agreement between the nuclear powers on (a) no test in any environment, (b) moratorium on PNE's and (c) using NTM for verification. "Direct consultation have also been proposed for resolving the question of compliance, for on-site inspection by agreement... There is a clear basis for formulating a treaty and, pending its elaboration, we see no reason why the three governments which have already provided evidence of their political will, cannot agree forthwith, bilaterally or unilaterally, to moratorium on nuclear weapon testing in future." [51]

India also felt that time was ripe for CD to involve itself in drafting the text of the treaty including issues of duration, withdrawal, ratification etc.

P.V. Narasimha Rao, the then Minister for External Affairs, said at the UN General Assembly's Second Special Session on Disarmament on June 11, 1982:

"How can this session follow up the declaration of first session ? I venture to propose the following concrete programme of action.

...immediate, suspension of all nuclear weapons tests." [52]

In 1984, India alongwith five other nations of Argentina, Greece, Mexico, Sweden and Tanzania appealed for a halt to nuclear testing in what was caled the "Six Nation Initiative". In January 1985, the heads of the six nations met in New Delhi at the invitation of the then Prime Minister, Rajiv Gandhi, and declared that "two specific steps today require special attention: The prevention of arms race in outer space and a comprehensive test ban treaty."

In a speech at the same six-nation Summit, Rajiv Gandhi said, "Existing compacts deny to non-nuclear weapon states the right to conduct experiments even for peaceful purposes, while placing no restraint on the nuclear weapon powers in the matter of multiplying their arsenals. This is a discrimination to which we have objected."[53]

Giving details, he said later in that year, "We, the co-authors of the six-nation initiative, have gone beyond merely pleading for disarmament. We have made a specific proposal for a 12-month moratorium on all nuclear weapon tests.... Furthermore, we have offered to monitor the implementation of the moratorium through our own monitoring stations... We look forward with some anticipation to the resumption of the negotiations in Geneva in January. We have no illusions but we do harbour the hope that the people's yearning for a secure and lasting peace will find reflections at the negotiating table." [54] The leaders sought a moratorium on testing of nuclear weapons for a 12-month period beginning January 1986. Following up this initiative, the foreign ministers of the Coordinating Bureau of Non-Aligned Countries, who met in Delhi in April 1986, issued a call for nuclear disarmament. It called upon USA to stop nuclear testing and requested USSR to continue restraint on these tests until an agreement was reached on test ban or at least until the next meeting of the heads of the two powers took place.

Speaking in February 1986, the Indian representative, Eric Gonsalves , said in the CD that the opponents of CTBT put two arguments. One was security advantage vis-a-vis the adversary, of securing modernization and non-obsolescence of existing weapons. Secondly, reference had been made to the perceived disadvantage of the state parties to a future test-ban treaty in the event of evasion by others. As for the first question, he said, "we do not see how carrying out more tests is essential, especially when the existing nuclear weapons with the superpowers are, on each side's admission, adequate to deter the adversary."

On the second issue he said, "The efficiency of national and international seismic monitoring arrangements is by objective international standards adequate for effective verification and can very easily be upgraded." Besides, "political commitment of the international community as a whole to a comprehensive nuclear weapon test ban will in itself be an effective deterrent against attempts to go in for evasion." [55]

In 1986, the Indian representative, Narayanan said that CTBT claimed the "highest priority" in the concrete programme for nuclear disarmament. He added that "we are unable to accept the view that a test ban can be considered only after deep and substantial reductions in nuclear forces have been made. Both aspects can and must be tackled simultaneously since as long as nuclear testing facilitates the sophistication of arsenals the results can only be sophisticated escalation rather than reversal of the process of arms race." [56]

He said that India was not convinced of the validity of the argument that verification constituted an obstalce in the way of conducting comprehensive test ban treaty "particiularly as on-site inspections have been offered to supplement the national technical means to verify compliance to a test ban... Besides the six nations themselves have offered their considerable technical expertise on monitoring such nuclear tests."

In any case, according to him, India believed that the issue of test ban "should be addressed in an ad hoc committee of this conference which should be constituted with an appropriate negotiating mandate without further delay...Refusal to establish such a subsidiary body would be a negative development showing the absence of political will."[57]

At the ministerial meeting of the Coordinating Bureau of Non-Aligned Countries in New Delhi on 16 April 1986, the then Prime Minsiter Rajiv Gandhi said, "Nuclear escalation must be staunched at the source. This is why, more than 30 years ago, Jawaharlal Nehru was the first statesman to appeal for the suspension of nuclear tests, pending the conclusion of a comprehensive test ban treaty. The appeal remains unheeded as the world drifts closer to the edge of the abyss. A moratorium on all nuclear weapons test by all nuclear powers is essential."[58]

In a speeech at second Summit meeting of the Six-Nation Five-Continent Initiative on Peace and Disarmament at Ixtapa on 7 August 1986, he said, "Unfortunately, nuclear testing continues. It is contended that a ban on tests is not feasible in the absence of a mechanism for verification which would inspire confidence. That is why our six nations have put forward a proposal to undertake the verification of a moratorium. Our geographic reach, technology competence and independence of bloc rivalries should command acceptance." [59]

In his speech at the Eighth Summit of Non-Aligned Movement on 2 September 1986 at Harare, Rajiv Gandhi remarked:

"We have urged an immediate moratorium on all nuclear tests. The problem of verification has been raised. We have, therefore, placed our extensive technical expertise and global geographic reach at the disposal of the international community to verify cessation of nuclear testing. The Soviet Union responded with a unilateral moratorium, extended three times, most recently in the wake of Mexico Declaration. We seek a similar response from the other nuclear-weapon powers." [60]

In his inaugural speech at the Internatioonal Seminar on "Non-Alignment and World Peace", New Delhi on 7 August 1987, Rajiv Gandhi stated, "The prospects for nuclear disarmament are better now than they have been for many years. After Reykjavik and subsequent proposals, what we need is a moratorium on nuclear tests to facilitate progress in the disarmament negotiations." [61] In 1987 India reiterated its demand for halt in "testing by all states in all environments for all time." It also repeated its earlier proposal to establish an ad hoc committee on a nuclear test ban "to initiate the multilateral negotiations of a treaty for the prohibition of all nuclear weapon test." [62] It severely criticized the proposal for setting up an ad hoc committee without a negotiating mandate. Reiterating this, Natwar Singh, said in the subsequent CD session, "We remain unpursuaded that non-negotiating mandate for the ad hoc committee on a nuclear test ban would in any way facilitate or bring us any closer to realizing the goal of a treaty prohibiting all nuclear weapon tests." [63]

In 1988, Prime Minister Rajiv Gandhi, while addressing the Third Special Session of the United Nations General Assembly on Disarmament called for a moratorium on testing of all nuclear weapons and initiation of negotiations for a comprehensive test ban treaty in the first stage of the "Action Plan" for achieving the goal of a nuclear-weapon free and and non-violent world order (Stage I (1988-1994), clause 2.9 VI and 2.1 a VII). The "Action plan" thus presented envisaged "Entry into force of a Comprehensive Test Ban Treaty" in Stage II (1995 to 2000 AD) as per clause 2.2 a.(iv). [64]

Speaking in the First Committee of the UN General Assembly on 17 October 1991, Atal Bihari Vajpayee, Member of Parliament, observed:

"The Ad hoc Committee on a Nuclear Test Ban, which India had the honour to chair, was reestablished this year, but once again without a full-fledged mandate to negotiate a nuclear test ban treaty. In this connection, India welcomes the unilateral moratorium on the testing of nuclear weapons which has been proposed by President Gorbachev. We invite all nuclear weapon States to announce similar moratorium. We would strongly urge that the Ad Hoc Committee on a Nuclear Test Ban is reestablished next year with positive negotiating mandate" [65]

Speaking at the First Committee again next year (1992), Vajpayee said,

"We are encouraged that an early conclusion of such

a Treaty is now advocated not only by the Russian Federation but also by several other countries in Europe. We welcome the decision of the Russian Federation and France to observe a limited moratorium on nuclear weapon tests as well as further constraints on nuclear testing approved by the US Legislature. It is important that all nuclear weapon states respond positively to these announcements of unilateral moratoria, thereby creating a positive environment for negotiations to be undertaken for a Nuclear Test Ban Treaty in the Conference on Disarmament. It is our earnest hope that the Conference on Disarmament will arrive at a consensus at the beginning of its 1993 session on the modalities of such negotiations."[66]

The Indian position on the eve of cosponsoring the resolution on CTBT was explained by the Ambassador at CD, Satish Chandra thus: "A comprehensive test ban treaty has a very important place among all the measures envisaged in the context of nuclear disarmament. Indeed, as one commentator put it, a CTBT is 'the most sought-after and most elusive of arms control measures of the nuclear age.' The international political climate today presents a golden opportunity to the international community to put once and for all an end to nuclear-weapon testing. Let it not be said that we have once again failed to seize it."[67] Giving details of India's position, Satish Chandra said:

"The scope of the comprehensive test-ban treaty has been clearly spelt out in the preamble of the PTBT of 1963, which recognized that its objective was to seek to achieve the discontinuance of all tests on nuclear weapons for all times. In our view, therefore, a treaty on nuclear test ban, which would be comprehensive in character, should have three essential characteristics, namely, (i) it should cover all states including the five nuclear-weapon states, (ii) it should extend the prohibition on the testing of nuclear weapons to the underground environment as well; and (iii) it should do so for all time. The verification system to be developed must be non-discriminatory in character in the sense of providing equal rights and obligations to the state parties to the proposed treaty including equal access. The aim of the CTBT and consequently its scope should be to prevent the testing of nuclear weapons and thereby to inhibit in a non-discriminatory way proliferation of nuclear weapons in their horizontal as well as vertical dimension. It cannot be conceived as an instrument designed to curtail technological progress or to perpetuate the division of the world into two categories of nations. In the promotion of achievement of a nuclear test ban, the interests of the nuclear weapon states must be taken into account on the basis of complete equality with the interests of the non-nuclear-weapon States.

"A compelling reason why CTBT has become a matter of high priority is to prevent the development of 'third generation' nuclear weapons. It would, of course, at the same time help reduce the chances of horizontal proliferation. In our view, a comprehensive test-ban treaty would go a long way in arresting the nuclear arms race and bringing to an end the development of more lethal warheads. We hope that all the nuclear-weapon States will respond positively to President Clinton's announcement and engage purposefully in multilateral negotiations for an effective and verifiable comprehensive test-ban treaty, which has long been a goal of international disarmament community. Any limited bilateral or regional approach to this issue which concerns all states would be inappropriate, and accordingly, a comprehensive test-ban treaty should be negotiated multilaterally."

The stand was reiterated in the First Committee, when the Indian representative M.M. Jacob said on 25 October 1993:

"India is heartened by the historic decision of the Conference on Disarmament on August 10,1993 to give its Ad hoc Committee on Nuclear Test Ban a negotiating mandate. We believe that CTBT would go a long way in arresting the nuclear arms race and bringing to an end the development of more lethal warheads. Another compelling reason why CTBT has become a matter of high priority is to prevent the development of 'third generation nuclear weapons'. The aim of CTBT and consequently its scope should be to prevent the testing of all nuclear weapons and thereby to inhibit in a non-distrimantory way proliferation of nuclear weapons in their horizontal as well as vertical dimsnesions. It must not, however, be conceived as an instrument designed to curtail technological progress or to perpetuate the division of the world in `haves' and `haves not'. Accordingly the CTBT should be non-discriminatory in character in the sense of providing equal rights and obligations to the State parties of the proposed treaty including equal access. India looks forward to the early commencement of multilateral negotiations for an effective and verifiable CTBT and to its conclusion in 1994."[68]

Post-1993 Developments

Draft Treaty

Preamble : Indian response is being dealt with here on issue by issue basis. As far as Indian opposition to Preamble is concerned, it opposes any reference to NPT in the preamble. Speaking in September 1994, India's representative Satish Chandra said, "since we are not a signatory to the NPT, any reference to the same would not be acceptable to us."[69]

Speaking in September 1995, Ms. Arundhati Ghose, the Indian representative said, "... the preamble of the treaty will have to clearly define the linkage of the CTBT to the overall framework of nuclear disarmament."

In a working paper introduced in January 1996 India proposed following changes ("new language") to be incorporated into the preamble of the treaty:[70] as para 2 bis (New):

> 'Convinced that cessation of nuclear weapon testing within the framework of an effective nuclear disarmament process in the interest of mankind.'

In para 2 it suggested:

> 'Convinced that the present international situation provided an opportunity to take further effective measures towards nuclear disarmament through the total elimination of nuclear weapons within a time-bound framework and against the proliferation of nuclear weapons in all aspects, and declining their intention to take such measures.'

Para 4:

> 'Affirming that the elimination of the nuclear threat and the attainment of a nuclear weapon free world have the highest priority, and in this context, requires the commitment of all states to take further measures within an agreed timeframe towards the total elimination of all nuclear weapons.'

Para 8:

> 'Convinced that the most effective way to achieve an end to nuclear testing is through conclusion of a universal and internationally and effectively verifiable comprehensive nuclear test ban treaty that will attract the adherence of all states and will contribute to the

prevention of the proliferation of nuclear weapons in all its aspects and will be an integral step in the time-bound process of nuclear disarmament and therefore to the enhancement of international peace and security.'

Para 13 bis(New)
'Emphasizing that the principal objective of this Treaty is to end the qualitative improvement and development of nuclear weapon systems.'

Scope : In July 1993 India said what the scope should aim at has been spelt out in the preamble of the PTBT of 1963, which recognized that its objective was to seek to achieve discontinuance of all tests of all nuclear weapons for all times. In India's view, therefore, a treaty on nuclear test ban which would be comprehensive in character should have three essential characteristics, namely, (i) it should cover all states including the five nuclear-weapon states; (ii) it should extend the prohibition on the testing of nuclear weapons to the underground environment as well; (iii) it should do so for all the time.

The aim of the CTBT and, therefore, its scope should be to prevent the testing of nuclear weapons and thereby to inhibit in a non-discriminatory way proliferation of nuclear weapons in their horizontal as well as vertical dimension.[71]

In June 1994, India reiterated this stand adding that "we believe that no test should be carried out under the pretext of safety purposes. The ban should not establish thresholds."[72]

Taking a cautious attitude towards preparatory activities, India's stand was: "We believe that we have to be careful when approaching the idea of banning preparatory activities. Preparations which make a nuclear weapon explosion imminent should certainly be within the scope of a CTBT; however research and scientific activity related to peaceful uses of nuclear energy should not be unnecessarily targeted. It is essential, therefore, to examine the aspect further and work out a clear definition of preparatory activity that needs to be covered."

In September 1994, after "closely examining" the various views expressed on "preparations" to be included India said, "While inclusion of imminent preparations is laudable, defining the term is difficult, its verification would be costly. Accordingly we feel "preparations" need not be directly referred to in the article dealing with basic obligations."[73]

In April 1995, speaking on behalf of G-21 as its coordinator the Indian delegate, Satish Chandra said that G-21 had made it clear that the CTBT should be for complete cessation of nuclear tests by all in all environment. The ban should be comprehensive and no tests should be carried out under any pretext. The Group of 21 also noted with disappointment the stand taken by nuclear weapon states on 'Scope' in rolling text—CD/1273/ Rev. Their continued support to "exceptions" to nuclear tests has resulted in little progress on fundamental article. It raises question on their commitment to the CTBT and goes against the mandate of ad hoc committee.[74]

In June 1995, India put forward the following proposal to define the text in a working paper CD/NTB/WP 244. It said:

1. Each State Party undertakes to prohibit and to prevent and not to carry out any nuclear weapon explosion or any other nuclear test or any release of nuclear energy caused by the assembly or compression of fissile or fusion material by chemical explosive or other means, at any place under or beyond its jurisdiction or control.

2. Each State Party undertakes furthermore to refrain

from causing, encouraging or in any way participating in the carrying out of any nuclear weapon test explosion or any other nuclear explosion."

India had consulted with the rest of G-21 and found considerable support for submitting the text. But some non-nuclear weapon states were concerned that defining a nuclear explosion could complicate verification; others wanted explicit references to prohibit PNE's.

In September 1995 India reiterated this position.[75]

Speaking in January 1996, the Indian delegate came down heavily on laboratory testing saying, " As the PTBT drove testing underground, we do not wish the CTBT to drive testing into the laboratories by those who have the resources to do so." Criticising the plan to conduct "sub critical" tests, she said, "We must ensure that CTBT leaves no loopholes for activity either explosive based or non-explosive based, aimed at the continued development and refinement of nuclear weapons. Consequently, the political intent needs to be reflected in the CTBT, clearly defining our objective — a treaty which will bring an end to all nuclear weapons development, not constrained by artificial limits of verification."[76]

Verification: In September 1993, India said that the verification system to be developed must be non-discriminatory in character in the sense of providing equal rights and obligations to the state parties to the proposed treaty including equal access.[77]

In June 1994, a more detailed position was put forward in addition to reiterating the above stand. Accordingly, India stated: "We believe that seismic verification would form the core of a future verification regime. India had participated in GSETT-1 and GSETT-2 experiment and has committed to participate in GSETT-3 also and encourages more countries to participate in it in order to make the CTBT a technically verfiable treaty. We have considered the utility of some non-seismic techniques such as radionucleides and perhaps hydroacoustic, but are yet to be convinced of other non-seismic events." It further said, "On-site inspections should only serve the purpose to cover the gaps left by these methods and should be taken only if there is a substantive suspicion of violation."[78]

In September 1994, India stated that it favoured special monitoring arrangements for established nuclear weapon test sites and eventually some transparency norms could be negotiated.[79]

Talking about the verification system in general, India said that it did not favour the idea that those states that have accepted full-scope safeguards as part of their obligations under the NPT, need not accept all aspects of a CTBT verification regime. "At Present", it believed, that a cost-effective combination of seismic, radionucleide, hydroacoustic and infrasonic monitoring techniques would be adequate to verify a CTBT in the lower atmosphere, water and underground. It felt that a nuclear test explosion in outer space would require the use of EMP sensors, optical flash and fluorescent sensors and satellite monitoring. Inclusion of these techniques, it is felt, in a verification regime is questionable as it would provide only marginal utility in terms of assurance while enhancing the cost manifold.

Of the four verification techniques, an international seismic monitoring network was considered to be the most critical. Beside seismic stations offered for participation in GSETT-3, India also has some radionucleide monitoring stations which may be upgraded. For CTBT verification, radionucleide monitoring would extend to cover short-lived isotopses in particulate form and noble gases — Krypton and Xenon. India did not share the view that radionucleide monitoring be on-line because of the financial implications. Co-location of

INDIA'S RESPONSE

seismic stations with infrasound arrays should also be considered as a cost-effective measure. This would enable infrasonic data to be provided on-line. Regarding hydroacoustic monitoring, India had suggested a reduction in the number of moored stations by careful examination and by establishing some coastal seismic stations.

India felt that the Secretariat and the International Data Centre (IDC) should have the capability to both detect and discriminate between events. Many states did not have the capability to analyse large volumes of data. In India's veiw, daily IDC bulletins should be prefaced by an analytical summary. Any anomalous event should be brought to the attention of the Executive Council immediately. Of course, all states would enjoy access to IDC data to derive their own analysis and interpretation. In all cases, the IDC should play an analytical role and not be limited merely to data collection and dissemination.

India felt that on-site inspection would be the most intrusive element of the verification regime. This would be a necessary part of the verification regime for deterrence purposes as well. India visualized routine visits only for authentication purposes and an on site-inspection to be a rare event."[80]

In April 1995, speaking on behalf of G-21, Satish Chandra noted: "The G-21 feels that the vast technical material already prepared by experts on the subject in the past two years is a sufficient basis for delegations to take political decisions. There does not seem much merit in holding expert sessions. The experts could be part of their national delegations. The time has come now to take political decisions in order to achieve progress in external form in the rolling text." The group also said that the verification system should be cost-effective. Verification system should be non-discriminatory in character and guarantee equal access to all states. The technical secretariat should have the capacity and the responsibility of analysing the data received from the IMS. The Group did not agree with the emphasis placed by some delegations on their "national technical means" to judge an ambiguous event. The organization should be responsible for judgement in this regard. The Indian delegate to CD said, in September 1995, that the on-site inspections should be carried out in rare circumstances and in the least intrusive and cost-effective manner possible. India believed that the design of the regime should be geared to prevent it while at the same time realistically retaining its effectiveness. Accordingly, India felt that the request for the on-site inspection should be based on IMS data. Full opportunity should be provided to the state party to be inspected to assist in clarifying the situation through a mandatory consultation and clarification procedure. The Executive Council should thoroughly examine the request and have a decision by three-forths majority of members on whether or not the OSI is warranted. A managed access regime should operate during the on-site inspection to maintain a balance between the rights and obligations of the state party being inspected.[81]

Speaking in September 1995, the Indian delegate said that verification system should be universal, non-discriminatory and should guarantee equal access to all states. India's view was that the International Data Centre working as an integral part of the Technical Secretariat should have the capacity to receive, assess and analyse data from the International Monitoring System. The judgement of non-compliance should be the responsibility of the organization.

On-site inspections would have to be approved by the Executive Council after due consideration and in an appropriate time framework, in which provision should be made for obligatory consultation and clarification to clarify the ambiguity.[82]

India sought a cost-effective system in September 1994. India stated that the system should be cost-effective so that the capital, operational and maintenance costs of the system did not result in an unreasonable burden to the concerned State Parties. The cost-effectiveness and the degree of confidence provided by a typical verification system ought to be optimized so that the CTBT could enjoy universal adherence.

Speaking on behalf of G-21, Indian delegate Satish Chandra said that the cost of the organization's activities including verifications should be borne by the State Parties in accordance with the UN scale of assessments adjusted to take into account differences in membership between the United Nations and the organization of the CTBT.[83]

In September 1994 the Indian delegate stated that it believed that a CTBT organization, "preferably a separate specific organization, should serve the purpose of implementation of the CTBT verification regime. The CTBT organization should have the capability of analyzing and exchanging both international seismic data and other non-seismic data."[84]

Organization : India held that the organization should consist of a Conference of State Parties, an Executive Council and a technical secretarial (excluding the IDC). India has suggested that a scientific advisory group may be constituted to provide independent and relevant inputs to the Executive Council.

In September 1995, Indian Ambassador to CD. Ms. Arundhati Ghose, said that responses to questionnaires to IAEA for the seat of the organization "will facilitate our decision making process". India held that non-compliance should be the responsibility of the organization.[85]

Entry into Force (EIF) : India favours a treaty which

should attract universal adherence. Stating this in June 1994 it held that "it (EIF) should not be complicated to delay the process. EIF should come into being once ratification has been effected by a 'reasonable and representative' group of countries."

In September 1994, India held that the requirement of *ratification* by nuclear-weapon states only was too limited and that by the entire conference would unnecessarily delay the EIF of the CTBT. The Indian delegate to CD said, "Certain other countries which are key to the success of a universal and non-discriminatory CTBT must be included at the outset. We therefore believe that EIF should be based on ratification by a reasonable and representative group of countries." [86]

Repeating the argument in April 1995, (speaking on behalf of the G-21) the Indian delegate, Satish Chandra, expressed the hope of the group that the CTBT should be able to attract universal adherence. He said, "EIF made contingent upon ratification by the nuclear-weapon states would make the CTBT hostage to them as well as a discriminatory treaty. The expansion of CD membership should also not be utilized as a pretext to delay the EIF." [87]

In January 1996, India moved a proposal (working paper) stating the language on entry into force. It stated that "notwithstanding anything contained in this Article, this treaty shall enter into force only after all state parties have committed themselves to the attainment of the goal of total elimination of all nuclear weapons within a well-defined framework (of ten years.)" [88]

Duration and Review of Treaty : In September 1994, India said that the treaty should be of unlimited duration. India also supported periodic review of the treaty. As for decision making and substantive issues in the EC, it should be on the basis of a two-thirds majority, present and voting.[89]

INDIA'S RESPONSE

In January 1996, India proposed a working paper on review. It stated, "Ten years after entry into force of this treaty, or earlier if so suggested by the two-thirds majority of State Parties to the treaty by submitting a proposal to this effect to the depository, a conference of state parties will be held to review the operation of the treaty and with a view to ensuring that the objectives, purpose and the provisions of the Preamble of the treaty are being realized. Such a review shall take into account any new scientific and technological developments relevant to the treaty." [90]

Global Elimination

In June 1994, India held that the only credible guarantee against the use or threat of use of nuclear weapon lay in elimination of such weapons. "We, however, recognize that complete nuclear disarmament is a complex issue. Therefore, pending the elimination of nuclear weapons, it is for the nuclear-weapon states to provide all security assurances to non-nuclear weapon states against the use or threat of use of nuclear weapons in an internationally and legally binding form i.e. universal and without any qualification or discrimination." Therefore it favoured an instrument based on the "common formula" approach. "In the first stage of our action plan, we advocated conclusion of a convention to outlaw the use of threat or use of nuclear weapons pending their elimination as a measure collateral to nuclear disarmament".[91]

In September 1994, India suggested (in regard to Preamble) that a clear linkage to nuclear disarmament and elimination of nuclear weapons should be established. It added that norm of non-proliferation and disarmament should be strengthened by a non-use agreement.

Speaking specifically on behalf of the Indian delegation, (who had earlier spoken on behalf of the G-21), Satish

Chandra said in April 1995 that India had consistently taken the position that the only credible guarantee against the use or threat of use of nuclear weapons lay in global elimination of such weapons. "We, however, realise that complete nuclear disarmament is a complex issue. Accordingly, pending the complete elimination of nuclear weapons, it is imperative that the nuclear-weapon states provide unconditional security assurances to all non-nuclear weapon states, irrespective of whether or not they were NPT signatories, against the use or threat of use of nuclear weapons in a multilaterally negotiated and legally binding form i.e. universal and without any qualification or discrimination."

He said, "It is unfortunate that the new draft resolution of the UN Security Council did not meet this objective. In fact it was weaker than the Security Council resolution 255 which required categorical and immediate action by the United Nations in case of aggression involving nuclear weapons or threat of such aggression against non-nuclear weapon state, irrespective of whether or not it was party to the NPT. He said that provisions relating to security assurances has been left vague and were open to interpretation.[92]

The first indications of "change" were seen in the address of AEC chairman, Dr. R. Chidambaram to the 39th General Conference of the IAE in September 1995. He said, "The recent nuclear tests carried out by some States, which are parties to the NPT, soon after its indefinite extension, highlight the inherent defects of the Treaty. These developments will have repercussions on the Comprehensive Nuclear Test Ban Treaty(CTBT). We see CTBT as a step towards nuclear disarmament, but CTBT will be meaningful only if it is linked firmly to the total elimination of all nuclear weapons within a well-defined time framework, say within the next ten years. In our considered view, there is a pressing need for such a disarmament regime which is universal, comprehensive and non-discriminatory. A sincere attempt to reach towards this goal is conspicuous now by absence."[92a]

Speaking around the same time during the 50th Anniversary celebration (25 September to 12 October) of the United Nations, Mr. Pranab Mukherjee, the then External Affairs Minister said that he was "glad" that a CTBT was being negotiated, but "we also note that nuclear weapon states have agreed to a CTBT only after acquiring the know-how to develop and refine their arsenals without the need for tests. In our view, the CTBT must be an integral step in the process of nuclear disarmament. Development of new warheads or refining existing ones after a CTBT is in place, using innovative technologies, would be as contrary to the spirit of the CTBT as the NPT is to the spirit of non-proliferation. CTBT must contain commitments to further measures within an agreed time-frame towards the creation of a nuclear weapon free world," [92b]

In the statement issued on 21 September 1995, India did not mention that it was not co-sponsoring the resolution it had hitherto been doing. The linkage between the treaty and disarmament were more clearly spelt out. The delegate said:

> "International negotiations on nuclear issues were being carefully monitored, and nuclear disarmament is an issue on which Indian opinion is united. The CTBT and the proposed cut-off convention are seen as essential steps towards total nuclear disarmament. They are indeed (in our view) steps towards the eventual goal which will be meaningful only if they are linked firmly to the total elimination of nuclear weapons within a well defined framework. Otherwise they will be seen as narrow and futile exercises aimed only at controlling non-nuclear weapon states,

further strengthening the discrimination inherent in the non-proliferation regimes which exist today. India is committed to the CTBT and has been participating constructively in the negotiations with the aim of an early and successful conclusion of the treaty.

"India has long believed and continues to believe that the only answer to nuclear threat is the complete elimination of nuclear weapons. We understand that this cannot be done overnight and should be done in phased and time-bound framework. This demand has been seen unrealistic and idealistic on the grounds that nuclear weapons cannot be disinvented. This we feel is a disingenuous argument." [93]

In a statement on 25 January 1996, the Indian delegate Ms. Arundhati Ghose presented the viewpoint of her country in the following words:

"We are of the view that the treaty should be securely anchored in the global disarmament context and be linked through treaty language to the elimination of all nuclear weapons in a time-bound framework.

"We are not unaware that these states undertook 'to make progressive efforts to reduce nuclear weapons globally with the ultimate aim of eliminating these weapons. But we are justified in our scepticism as this undertaking was followed by reassertion of some of these countries citing reasons of their security, of their continuing need not only to possess these weapons but to ensure their reliability for use. Other developments including renouncing of 'sub-critical' tests for the refinement of the nuclear weapons, and proposals for political discussions on the future role of nuclear weapons to ensure the security of some nuclear-weapon states and their allies, and the inconsistency of these developments with the avowed goal of nuclear disarmament, have been noted by us with great unease.

INDIA'S RESPONSE

"Given the possibility of tr eating the perpetuating of the NPT as providing an indefinite license for the possession of nuclear weapons, it becomes even more imperative to have a legally binding commitment to eliminate these weapons in a specific time-frame."[94]

In a statement at the CD on February 26, India regretted that no progress had been reached on disarmament. The Indian Ambassador, Ms. Arundhati Ghose, dispelled the myth that life in the CD began with the indefinite extension of the NPT in May 1995 and that all mandate must flow from that conference. The conference draws its mandate from the consensus forged in first special session on Disarmament. The UN General Assembly in 1993 enjoyed the support of the entire international community, "something that the NPT does not."

On "time-bound" framework, Ms. Ghose said the Intermediate Nuclear Forces treaty (INF), START I and START II have inherent time frames. "The open-ended commitment to eliminate nuclear weapons is an unsigned promissory note, useless against threat of nuclear weapons", she said.

Another "misinterpretation" India thought was regarding the CD itself. It was being argued that CD was not the appropriate forum for negotiations on nuclear disarmament since the process would involve bilateral trade-offs, specialized verification, etc. "We cannot be part of actual trade-offs, since we have nothing to trade", she added.

She continued, "We see discussions in Ad hoc committee resulting in series of treaties with time-frames for the negotiations: one such step could be a convention prohibiting use or threat of those nuclear weapons. It could codify the legal norm against the use of nuclear weapons."[95]

Speaking on the same lines, the Indian foreign secretary, Mr. Salman Haider in his statement on 21 March 1996 said: "We believed them (at the start in 1950s) and we are even more convinced that CTBT should bring about a halt to the qualitative development, upgradation and improvement of nuclear weapons and should also mark the first irreversible step towards genuine nuclear disarmament within a time-bound framework"[95a]

India regretted that no consensus was reached on its formal proposal (made alongwith other members of Group of 21) for establishment of an Ad Hoc committee on nuclear disarmament to commence negotiations on a phased programme of nuclear disarmament for the eventual elimination of nuclear weapons within a specified framework of time. Mr. Haider also said: "we do not believe that acquisition of nuclear weapons is essential for national security and we have followed a conscious decision in this regard." [95b]

India Rejects CTBT Draft

In the May-June 1996 session of the Conference on Disarmament, India rejected the draft CTBT as it stood on June 20. India's stand has not seen any major change as this study goes to press.

The decision of rejection was announced at the CD by its Ambassador Ms. Arundhani Ghose and in New Delhi by the Foreign Secretary, Mr. Salman Haider. They said that India could not subscribe to the Treaty in "its present form".

Ms. Ghose said that the preambular references to disarmament in the draft treaty were "weak and woefully inadequate". She added that despite India's efforts to place CTBT in a disarmament context through various proposals, "the scope only bans nuclear weapon test explosions... it is very narrow and does not fulfil the mandated requirement of the comprehensive ban."

On 'Entry into Force' requirement (India's ratification of the Treaty being essential), she said, "We do not accept any language in the treaty that would affect our sovereign right to decide whether we should or should not accept the treaty."

Interestingly, this was the first time that security vis-a-vis neighbours was made in the context of nuclear weapons. Indirect references were made to China and Pakistan in both Ms. Ghose's and Salman Haider's statements. It was stated that India's capability demonstrated but as a matter of policy it had exercised restraint. "Countries around us continue their weapon programmes either openly or in a clandestine manner (Indirect reference to China and Pakistan, respectively). In such an environment India cannot accept any restraint on its capability if other countries remain unwilling to accept obligations to eliminate their nuclear weapons."[95c]

India also withdrew its offer of CTBT monitoring facilities. Subsequently, in response to a letter by the President of CD to all countries, which could have taken part in international monitoring system, in preparation for finalising monitoring facilities, Ms. Ghose requested that the references to monitoring facilities located in India be deleted from the draft text of the treaty.

Interestingly, the draft text then made 'entry into force' conditional on ratification by 44 countries (listed by IAEA) having research and power reactors. India has both and is included in the list.

Ms. Ghose said that going by the non-binding assurances in other treaties, India could only conclude that nuclear-weapon states were determined to continue to rely on nuclear weapons for their security and visualise the CTBT not as a serious disarmament measure but merely as instrument against horizontal proliferation. "The present CTBT is shaped more by technological preferences of nuclear-weapon states rather than by imperatives of nuclear disarmament. This cannot be the CTBT that India can be expected to accept"[95d]

India, it was stated, had based its assessments on the post-cold war doctrines of nuclear weapon states which justified use of nuclear weapons "against chemical or biological attack, or in a sub strategic role." Nuclear weapons "were being sought as a precaution against future erratic behaviour or threat from unspecified states, added Mr. Ghose."

Nuclear Debate

As far as the present debate in the country is concerned, the viewpoints can be placed in two categories: (i) Those supporting the idea of signing the treaty or "pro-signers"—the degree of emphasis for signing, however varies; (ii) Those opposing the idea of signing the treaty or "anti-signers". These two categories in turn have sub-categories. The former includes "die hard" signers and the "conditional" signers. Among the anti-signers are (a) those who think India should instead, continue testing—the "testers"; (ii) and those who think India should block the treaty—the "blockers"; and (iii) those who think India should withdraw from the treaty—the "withdrawalists".

The Pro-Signers

Among the "pro-signers" also the degree of support for signing the treaty varies. There is one group of experts, the "die-hard" signers who believe that the treaty is a worthy, "eminently desirable" goal. Their argument is: "New Delhi hardlined its stance in late January not because of change in ground reality , nor even because of NPT extension but for reasons that are widely seen as related to a strategy of "larger bargain" means at best and to devious maneuvers at worst. A larger bargain is a deal that goes beyond a CTBT and hence is, strictly speaking exterior to it."

According to this argument, India should modify its all-inclusive stand on scope and linkage and secure a no-loopholes zero-yield treaty that bans all nuclear weapon test explosions. Insistence on covering all tests "which involve a release of nuclear energy" is dysfunctional. A group of Plutonium sitting on a work bench also releases energy.

The proponents of this argument also feel that it is wrong to make the CTBT conditional upon a commitment to time-bound disarmament even in the treaty preamble. "Preamble deals with objectives and goals and not means or procedures of achieving them." It is argued that it would be ideal if New Delhi extracts a commitment from the nuclear weapon states to discuss a treaty for the elimination of nuclear weapons, along the lines of the Chemical Weapon Convention. "But there should not be a pre-condition. A CTBT is desirable in and of itself.

Besides, the argument goes, it is ludicrous to equate a one-line commitment, however binding, with a 100-page long treaty with elaborate and precise definitions of prohibitions, obligations and verification, entry into force, monitoring, organisation, etc.

The CTBT's real significance, it is argued, "is that it will end the nuclear arms race, one of the most menaces the world has ever known. India strongly supports a fissile ban, which is also a freeze measure; if it adopts double standards on CTBT, it will only lose credibility."[96]

Another variant in the "pro-signers" group has following arguments to make":

(i) It caps nuclear arsenals of weapon powers; it improves India's security environment.

(ii) It is surely logical to try to reduce the uncertainties by limiting the arsenals of potential adversaries. Not to do so would mean perpetually having to upgrade "minimum deterrence" with all our present handicaps.

If India does not sign the CTBT, in reality the combination of moral and *realpolitik* factors which inhibited it from testing weapons in the past will continue to have the same force as before.

If India blocks a true zero-yield test ban because of absence of disarmament time-table, it allows the weapon powers to go on refining their weapons and increase the cost of maintaining India's own option at credible level.[97]

According to another view, the *"Scientist opinion"*, "During the last two decades when the concerned scientists in the US and in USSR were campaigning to end the Nuclear arms race, India's nuclear Ayatollahs were begging New Delhi to speed up its N-programme. From the very beginning of Nehru and Bhabha times, our nuclear policy has been shrouded in secrecy. No scientific body, not even Indian National Science Academy or Congress had even discussed the question of a sane nuclear policy.... No major scientists in India had raised a critical voice against N-arms race in the Indian subcontinent."

The proponents of this view feel that India "must restore its international leadership against nuclear weapons and join the world nations in making the five rogue nuclear-weapon states respect the scientific opinion and conclude the CTBT without further delay."[98]

Then there are others, the "conditional signers" who think if some of the basic requirements of India are met, it should accede to the CTBT. These are:

(i) It should be truly comprehensive in that it should cover all tests - a real zero yield CTBT.

INDIA'S RESPONSE

(ii) It should not be discriminatory in that it should leave no loopholes for nuclear-weapon powers to go on testing. India should, therefore, seek to eliminate laboratory tests through computer simulation in which nuclear-weapon powers have a decisive advantage.

(iii) It must contain a clause rejecting nuclear weapons as a basis of security and unambiguously accepting the objective of eliminating the weapons.

(iv) Whether it should have a time target for elimination should be a subject of negotiation. Elimination as an ultimate objective has no operational significance. India should, therefore, try to get the notion of a time target accepted even if exact dates may not be agreed upon. In any case, India should try to reach an agreement for commencing without delay negotiations on elimination in the appropriate forum, that is, the Conference on Disarmament.[99]

The Anti-Signers

The "anti-signers" are more sharply categorized since they have specific reason, each differing with the other. Taking these one by one:

The "testers" argue that Washington seemed to have timed the campaign about India conducting a second test to embarrass New Delhi first before the CTBT Conference in Geneva and then after its failure to make India change its stance.

It is argued that testing could become necessary soon to cope with emerging nuclear realities. Ideally a credible weapons capability should have been developed much earlier; the costs would have become bearable by now. The ambiguity about the state of Indian programme has yielded no lasting benefit. It tends to fuel wild speculation while the actual preparation may not be nearly so decisive as claimed by foreign critics or smugly hinted at by Indian spokesmen. New Delhi has little to lose by making an open statement of intent to develop the technical competence to support it.

The proponents of this view argue that a reversal of India policy is not pragmatic. On the contrary, the nuclear option will have to be strengthened if necessary by testing. While there is no question of accepting the CTBT, in present circumstances, the treaty could possibly be signed, when it comes into force in a few year's time if credible weapons capability can be built up in the meantime with an adequate number of tests. India can do this by remaining outside NPT or after declaring itself a nuclear power and then claim privileges reserved for nuclear weapon states.[100]

The Withdrawalists

According to the 'withdrawalists' it is now abundantly clear that the CTBT will not be comprehensive, universally applicable or a step towards disarmament. Even the claim of the nuclear-weapon powers and their camp followers that it will prevent new nuclear weapon states from emerging has been disproved. They say that the CTBT is in any case superfluous when 178 nations have voluntarily abjured nuclear weapons, and, by implication, nuclear testing. Any proliferation in future will be not by development of nuclear weapons and their testing by new weapon powers but by clandestine transfer of weapons from nuclear-weapon powers to their chosen clients.

They believe that those who argue in favour of India fighting the CTBT, clause by clause, tend to take the treaty more seriously than it deserves. India should fight for a genuine comprehensive test ban. But so long as the NPT remains breached there is no way in which a meaningful comprehensive test ban can be achieved.

Therefore, fighting in the CD for a comprehensive test ban is futile. There was some justification in entertaining hopes on India bringing about a true comprehensive test ban treaty before the breach of Articles I and III of the NPT became public knowledge. But not after that.

They argue, "Therefore India should declare the CTBT has no meaning in the light of the new developments. Since the NPT has been indefinitely and unconditionally extended there is no possibility of repairing the breaches of Articles I and III of the Treaty. In any case the breach of Articles I and III of the NPT, and consequent loss of purpose of the CTBT are of immediate relevance to Indian security since that transaction has taken place between two of India's nuclear neighbours. In these circumstances India should withdraw from the CTBT negotiations after citing these reasons. Such a withdrawal will shift the focus to China's action and Sino-Pakistan nuclear relationship." [101]

The Blockers

The 'Blockers' argue that the challenge posed by the CTBT continues to be simplistically portrayed in the national debate as a 'sign' or 'not to sign' issue. That issue will face India only if there is consensus agreement at the Conference on Disarmament on the final form and shape of a CTBT. Any agreement will require India's support since each of the CD's current 37 member-stats enjoys effective veto power. The real issue is whether India will employ that power to frustrate the efforts of the nuclear powers to create a CTB, not to comprehensively outlaw all forms of testing, but with comprehensive loopholes for their benefits.

According to them if India allows a monster to be born in Geneva, it will be repeating the mistake of the 1960s when the NPT was permitted to emerge. The new monster would be more ruthless than the old, and the costs of staying out of the CTB could be higher than the costs of staying out of the NPT. India's vital interests will be gravely damaged if it did not block a flawed CTB but later stayed out of it. Such a course will yield little security advantage since an internationally isolated India will not be able to test. Rather, it will open the path to a discriminatory fissile material cut-off and set in motion the unravelling of the country's nuclear options. India has to employ its veto power to ensure that it gets a CTB compatible with its interests.[102]

Conclusions

Where does all this lead us to? The problem basically is in that aspect of thinking which considers "the government can do nothing right". Politically, it seems to have become the democratic norm just as the feudal norm was "the king can do nothing wrong."

It is true that India has been seeking a CTBT right from the Nehruvian days—1954 "Standstill Agreement". At that time it was a step towards disarmament and was to be adopted till elimination of nuclear weapons took place. Nehruvian "Never the Bomb" order was also the cause of his considering testing as "crime against humanity". That Shastri thought of conducting a test, "Subternnean Nuclear Explosion" (SNE) to be precise, in line with his "not now a bomb" is only a matter of debate, since we have it cited in Western sources.

But it is a fact that in mid-1960s India looked at CD seeking exceptions to peaceful nuclear explosions and was doing that till 1990.

Indira Gandhi's conducting of a peaceful nuclear explosion in 1974 and subsequent confusion created by Morarji's government were yet another phase of India's nuclear testing policy. Rajiv Gandhi sought test ban in two phases in his action plan.

But as for present, there is no denying the fact that India has become more categorical vis-a-vis "linkage". The Indian arguments on 'scope', 'verification', 'entry into force' are well in line with its open option policy.

The merit of this open option policy is not the scope of this study. Therefore, as for the present when an international treaty is being argued it is important to explain the Indian position clause by clause. If tomorrow there is an agreement on global elimination, India should not be found wanting in its position vis-a-vis nitty-gritties of the treaty.

Blocking the treaty at CD will "push" it to General Assembly, for the others (nuclear-weapon powers) will take it there. Nor will withdrawal help. North Korea's withdrawal from the NPT Extension Conference is a test case—no harm came to the extension process and no gain came to North Korea.

The present policy, therefore, is right on tracks. It does not ask you to make any compromise; it is in conformity with India's traditional policy. It is true that India is the target of the CTBT, Therefore "pro-signers" also do not have any merit in this argument.

What is being argued is that India should stay till the end, be firm and expound its position. For, it has to be remembered that India's nuclear policy has to respond to challenges and not be restricted to merely reacting to the big powers. So far as pressures are concerned, there will only be a marginal difference irrespective of the fact whether one is inside or outside the treaty.

As this study goes to the press there is a change in the EIF requirement. Earlier, it was the requirement that all the countries with monitoring stations should ratify it before EIF. After India's withdrawal of its monitoring facilities, the requirement (for EIF) is ratification by all countries having research and power reactors. This list includes India.

Clearly, all moves are being made to put pressure on India and attempts are being made to see somewhow or the other that it is roped in. Alternatively, India may be portrayed as a "spoiter".

There is loud thinking in the strategic community to block the treaty in order to resist coercion. Blocking would make sense only if India is prepared politically to take the challenge. Ideally India should stay out of the present treaty without blocking it and let others conclude it. For even if India blocks it, it could be taken to the UN General Assembly, where India would not have any such choice. The treaty would then go through and have a larger moral backing. Blocking, therefore, should be the 'last resort', i.e., if its name is not taken out of the list of countries required to ratify the treaty. For, then it would be a question of sovereignty. No country can be forced to sign a treaty unless defeated in war.

What is more important is that once CTBT comes into force it will be impossible to test. Equally important, irrespective of whether CTBT gets through or not, there are other moves on the horizon like the proposed Fissile Material Cut-off Treaty, which by virtue of more intrusive verification system, have much wider security implications (read threats) for India.

Notes and References

1. Parliamentary Debates, Vol.3, Part II, No.37, April 2,1954, col.3918.
2. UN Disarmament Commission Official Records (DCOR) Supplement for April, May and June 1954, DC/44 and Corr.1 pp.1-4.
3. DCOR for July, August & September, DC/54 p.1.
4. General Assembly Official Resolution,(GAOR), 10th Session, Document A/2949/Add1.

INDIA'S RESPONSE

5. UN General Assembly Official Records (UNGAOR), 9th session, First Committee, 770th Meeting, 26 October 1954, Ibid. 497th Plenary Meeting, November 4,1954.
6. GAOR, Ninth Session, Annex Agenda items 20 and 68, A/C. I/L.100 and Rev.1, pp.4-5.
6a. DCOR Supplement from April to December 1955, DC/71.
7. India and Disarmament, Ministry of External Affairs, New Delhi, 1988, p.54.
7a. Ibid p.78.
8. DCOR, 58th Meeting, July 12,1956, pp.16-18.
9. Ibid. pp.18-19, pp.26-27.
10. GAOR, 824th meeting, 21 January 1957, pp.59-60.
11. GAOR, Twelfth Session, 703rd Plenary meeting, October 8,1957, p.328.
12. Ibid, Agenda item 24/Document A/c I/L 176, Rev.4, November 1,1957, p.11.
13. GAOR, 716 Plenary Meeting, November 14, 1957, p.57 & GAOR 718th Plenary Meeting, Nov. 19,1957, p.466.
14. Keesings Contemporary Archives, 8-15 February 1958, p.16012A.
15. Soviet News, No.3743. December 14,1957, pp.185-6.
16. Department of State Bulletin No. 38, January 6, 1958, p.17.
17. GAOR, 14th Session Annexes Agenda item. Document A/C I/L. 238 Rev. 1, p.2.
18. Originally India submitted draft resolution A/C I/L 237; subsequently more countries joined and submitted revised version of their draft A/C I/L. 237/Rev.1 of A/C I/L 237/Rev 1/Addl.
19. GAOR, Document A/4186, August 17, 1959, p.1.
20. GAOR, 1057th Meeting, November 18,1959, pp. 163-4.
21. GAOR, 15th session, Annexes, Agenda item 67. 86, 69 and 73; Document A/4414, July 20,1960 pp.6-7.
22. Ibid. 1110th Meeting, 15th November 1960, p.137.
23. GAOR, 16th Session Annexes, Agenda item 73 and 72: Document A/4801/ Add.1, July 28,1961. pp.3-4.
24. ENDC/PV.5, March 20,1962, p.41.
25. Lok Sabha Debates, Series 2, Vol.61, Session 16, 1962, col.1014.

26. ENDC/PV.58, July 17,1962; ENDC/28, April 16,1962..
27. Lok Sabha Debates, Series 3, Vol.2, Session 1, 1962, col 2066-77.
28. ENDC/PV.78, September 3,1962 p.31
29. GAOR Seventeenth Session, Annexes Agenda item 77, Document A/5141 and Add1, pp.1-2.
30. Ibid. First Committee 1246th Meeting, October 10,1962, p.8
31. GAOR, 16th Session Explanatory Memorandum submitted by India on July 9,1962 A/5141/Add 1.
32. ENDC/PV.85, November 30,1962, p.24.
33. GAOR, Eighteenth Session Annexes, Agenda Item 73, Document A/5428, June 28,1963, pp.1-27.
34. UNGAOR, 18th session, Document A/5758.
35. Statement by the Foreign Minister Swaran Singh in Lok Sabha on thermonuclear explosion by China, May 10,1966.
36. Letter by Indian Permanent representative to the UN to all the permanent representatives, August 29,1966.
37. Statement by the Indian Representative Azim Hussain in the First Committee of the UN On November 28,1968 cited in JP Jain, Nuclear India, Vol. II (Radiant Publishers, 1974) p.222.
38. Statement by Indian representative in ENDC, May 23, 1969, (extract) cited in Ibid p.226.
39. Intervention by the Prime Minister Indira Gandhi in the Lok Sabha Debate, April 20,1970.
40. GAOR, First Committee, November 25,1970, A/C. I/L 546.
41. Written Answers of Prime Minister Mrs. Indira Gandhi in the Lok Sabha, 15 November,1972.
41a. Statement by Prime Minister Indira Gandhi in Rajya Sabha on November 15,1973 reproduced in Jain. n.37 p.332.
42. Government of India Press Note on the Nuclear Explosion, 18 May,1974, cited in JP Jain, Nuclear India, Vol. II, op cit. p.332.
43. CD/PV.78, 2 May 1978, p.15.
44. Ibid p.14.
45. CD/PV/47, 2 August 1979, p.26.
46. CD/PV/87, June 19, 1980, p.6
47. Ibid. p.7.

INDIA'S RESPONSE 217

48. CD/PV/97, July 31,1980, p.17
49. Text of the Speech at Special Session of the United Nations General Asembly, New York, June 9,1978, cited in *India and Disarmament, An Anthology of Selected Writings and Speeches* (Ministry of External Affairs) New Delhi,1988, p.,203.
50. Statement to *Trialogue*, a quarterly journal of the Trilateral Commission for North America-European Japanese Affairs, Fall 1982 cited in Ibid p.208.
51. CD/PV/95, July 31,1980, p.17.
52. See text of Speech reproduced in *India and Disarmament*, op.cit. 226
53. Text of the Speech at the Six nation Summit on Nuclear Disarmament, 28th January 1985.
54. Speech on Doordarshan, December 1985, in *India and Disarmament*, op.cit. p.240.
55. CD/PV/342, February 25,1986, pp.20,21
56. CD/PV/358, April 22,1986, p.7.
57. Ibid. p.10.
58. *India and Disarmament*, op.cit. 257.
59. Ibid. p.260.
60. Ibid. p.262.
61. Ibid, p.268.
62. CD/PV/207, February 26,1987, pp.4-6
63. CD/PV/408, April 23,1987, p.6.
64. Text of "Action Plan for ushering in a nuclear weapon free and non-violent order, " presented by the then Prime Minister of India, Rajiv Gandhi at III Special Session on Disarmament in June 1988.
65. Statment by Atal Behari Vajpayee, Member of Parliament in First Committee of the UN (Permanent Mission of India to the United Nations, New York), October 17,1991, p.5
66. Statment by Atal Behari Vajpayee, Member of Parliament in First Committee of the UN (Permanent Mission of India to the United Nations, New York), October 19,1992, pp.8-9.
67. CD/PV/657, September 3, 1993, pp 20-21.
68. Statment by Mr. M.M. Jacob, Member of Parliament in First Committee of the UN (Permanent Mission of India to the United Nations, New York), October 15,1993, p.4.

69. CD/PV/690/1, September 1, 1994, P.36
70. CD/NTB/WP.295, January 25, 1996.
71. CD/PV/657, September, 1993.
72. CD/PV/680, 2 June 1994, p.3
73. CD/PV/694, 1 September 1994.
74. CD/PV/705, 1 February 1995, p.32.
77. CD/PV/719, 21 September, 1995, p.6
76. Statement by Ambassador Arundhati Ghose at the Conference on Disarmament, Geneva, January 25,1996, p.5
77. CD/PV/657, September 3, 1993
78. CD/PV/680, 2 June 1994, p.4
79. CD/PV/690, 1 September 1994, p.34.
80. CD/PV/690, 1 September 1994, p.35.
81. CD/PV/705, April 6,1995 pp.32-33.
82. CD/PV/719, 21 September 1995, p.6
83. CD/1292; CD/NTB/WP 208; February 1,1995, p.2.
84. CD/PV/680, June 2,1994, p.4
85. CD/PV/719, 21 September 1995, p.6
86. CD/PV/690, 1st September 1994 pp.35-36.
87. CD/PV/705, 6 April 1995, p.33
88. CD/NTB/496, (page 63 of CD(1364) (Paper 3)
89. Cd/PV/690, 1st September 1994, p .36.
90. CD/NTB/WP/297, January 25, 1996.
91. CD/PV/680, June 2,1994, p .5
92. CD/PV/705, 6 April 1995, p.33.
92a. Address by Dr. R. Chidambaram, Chairman, Atomic Energy Commission and Leader of the Indian delegation of 39th General Conference of the international Atomic Energy Agency, Vienna, 18-22 September 1995, p.6.
92b. *Disarmament Times*, October 11, 1995, pp.2-3.
93. CD/PV/719, 2 September 1995, p.5
94. Statement by Arundhati Ghose to UN Office at Geneva in Conference on Disarmament, January 25,1996, p.2.
95. Statement by Arundhati Ghose to UN Office at Geneva in Conference on Disarmament on February 15,1996, pp.2-5

95a. Statement by Salman Haider, Foreign Secretary of India in the Plenary Meeting of Conference on Disarmament (Permanent Mission of India, March 21,1996). pp.1-2.
95b. Ibid p.3
95c. Ibid. p.6.
95d. Statement by Ambassador, Arundhati Ghose, Plenary Meeting of Conference on Disarmament (Permament Mission of India, June 20, 1996) p.1.
96. Praful Bidwai, 'The CTBT Issue-II:Accept Treaty and Move on', *Times of India*, Feburary 8,1996.
97. Amrita Abraham, 'Rethinking India's Strategy', *Indian Express*, March 14,1996.
98. Dhirendra Sharma, 'Scientists and CTBT', *Hindustan Times*, February 19,1996.
99. Muchkund Dubey, 'India's Nuclear Options', *Frontline*, 26 January 1996.
100. Amlendu Das Gupta, 'Nuclear Choice : Beyond Present Concerns', *Statesman*, March 5,1996.
101 K. Subramanyam, 'CTBT Negotiations: The Case for India's Withdrawal', *Times of India*, March 7,1996.
102. Brahma Chellaney, 'Should India Block or Stay out of a flawed CTBT', *Pioneer*, February 28,1996.

Epilogue

India has decided to block the draft comprehensive test ban treaty.The text presented by the Chairman, Ambassador Jaap Ramaker,is now considered as final. The Chinese changed stance— to make conduct of on-site inspections conditional on a demand by 30 members of the Executive Council—has been seen as a technical adjustment rather than an amendment. The Chinese had earlier demanded that the request should be made by two-thirds majority in the Executive Council, totalling 34. The Americans, on the other hand had put this number at 26—the simple majority.

The Indian decision to block the treaty was explained by India's permanent representative, Ms Arundhati Ghose, on 29 July 1996 at the Conference on Disarmament, Geneva. Stating that India's stand as explained on 20th June not to sign the treaty in this form stands for the same reasons mentioned at that time, she said, "Article XIV as it is presently drafted not only totally disregards my country's position we have found it unprecedented in treaty negotiating practice.Which country present here would accept a situation where after it has declared its dissatisfaction and, therefore its decision not to sign, much less ratify, a particular treaty finds that it is to be forced by other countries which accept the treaty to sign and ratify it despite it being against national interest or else face unspecified 'measures'?"

India proposed an ammendment on the lines of the Chemical Weapons Convention. It said, "This treaty shall enter into force 180 days after the date of the deposit of the instruments of ratification by 65 states and no less than two years after its opening for signature." If however,"the present text was sought to be retained", Ms. Ghosh informed the delegates that India "would be reluctantly obliged to object to this text being forwarded to the Plenary for consideration."